More QUILTS for BABY

That Patchwork Place®

Easy as ABC

Ursula Reikes

Credits

Editor-in-Chief . . . . Kerry I. Smith
Technical Editor . . . . Sally Schneider
Managing Editor . . . . Judy Petry
Design Director . . . . Cheryl Stevenson
Text and Cover Designer . . . . Cheryl Stevenson
Design Assistant . . . . Marijane E. Figg
Production Assistants . . . . Nancy Hodgson,
Copy Editor . . . . Liz McGehee
Proofreader . . . . Leslie Phillips
Illustrator . . . . Laurel Strand
Photographer . . . . Brent Kane

More Quilts for Baby: Easy as ABC
© 1997 by Ursula Reikes

Martingale & Company, 20205 144th Avenue NE
Woodinville, WA 98072-8478 USA

Printed in the United States of America
05 04   14 13 12 11

Library of Congress Cataloging-in-Publication Data

Reikes, Ursula,
    More quilts for baby: easy as ABC / Ursula Reikes.
        p. cm.
    ISBN 1-56477-187-3
    1. Quilting—Patterns. 2. Patchwork—Patterns. 3. Crib quilts.
I. Title.
TT835.R438 1997
746.46'041—dc21   97-1246
                                                            CIP

Dedication

For Trish Carey—Life is good!

Acknowledgments

Thank you to:

My husband, John, for his love and support, and his fabulous cooking;

My parents, Luise and Edward Golisz, for their unending faith in me;

The Editorial team at That Patchwork Place for encouraging me to do another book, and Sally Schneider for being an editor's editor;

Marion Shelton and Donna Lever for making their own creative versions of two of the quilts in this book;

Trish Carey, Kathryn Ezell, Kay Green, and Claudia L'Heureux for their help binding the quilts.

All the critters in my life for keeping me grounded and in touch with what is important.

And thank you to Fairfield Processing Corporation for providing Soft Touch cotton batting, to Madiera Rayon for providing their luscious rayon thread, and to In The Beginning Fabrics for their wonderful selection of fabrics.

Table of Contents

Introduction

Welcome to another book of colorful, simple quilts that can be made in an afternoon or an evening. My first book, *Quilts for Baby: Easy as ABC*, was published in 1993. Since then, I've received many letters from quilters all over the country, telling me how much they enjoyed making the quilts from my book. They couldn't believe how easy they were to make.

Many quilters discovered that the quilt patterns were not "just for baby." People made quilts for toddlers, teenagers, college students, friends, and loved ones. For example, Mary Mainwaring from Salem, Oregon, has made more than twelve quilts for family and friends from those patterns. Susanne Dunaway of Seattle, Washington, has made more than forty-five quilts for her favorite charities.

The most often-asked question in the letters was "When is your next book coming out?" Well, here it is! This book, like the first, was written for all those busy people who want to make something special, but don't have a lot of time to invest in the process. All the quilts in this book are simple to make, and most can be done in a short period of time.

I searched through several block dictionaries to find patterns that were easy to construct and that would accommodate the busy, bold fabrics I prefer. I looked for blocks that had a large area to feature a special fabric and that could be rotary cut and strip pieced. Twenty of the patterns in this book feature traditional blocks. Only one does not.

Many of the quilts in this book are larger than a standard crib-size quilt. While none are large enough to cover a bed, they can be used in a number of ways: to ward off the chill on a winter night, to snuggle under while reading or watching TV, to fold over the arm of a chair for a bright spot of color in a room, to take on a picnic for a summer outing. The possible uses are endless. It's also very easy to change the size of any of these quilts to suit your needs.

Be creative, have fun, experiment with different colors and prints. Consider wildlife prints for a nature lover, or a print with tool motifs for your favorite handyman. A quilt to say "thank you" or "I'm thinking of you" is easy with any of the patterns in this book. And don't worry about trying to match the decor of a room. Fun does not have to match anything.

General Directions

Anatomy of a Quilt

Backing: A large piece of fabric that covers the back of a quilt. For larger quilts, it may be constructed from more than one piece of fabric.

Batting: A layer inside the quilt, sandwiched between the quilt top and the quilt backing.

Binding: A strip of fabric, cut on either the straight of grain or the bias, sewn to and wrapped around the edges of the quilt to finish it.

Borders: The area surrounding the main body of the quilt top that acts like a frame on a picture. One or more fabric strips of varying widths may be added. *Borders with straight-cut corners* are applied in two steps: border strips are sewn to opposite side edges of the quilt top first, then to the top and bottom edges.

Borders with corner squares are applied in three steps: Border strips are sewn to opposite side edges of the quilt top first, then corner squares are sewn to each end of the remaining border strips. Finally, the border strips with corner squares attached are sewn to the top and bottom edges.

Corner Square: A square of fabric used to join adjacent border strips.

Cornerstone: A square of fabric used to join two sashing strips.

Half-Square Triangle Unit: A square made up of two right-angle triangles.

Quilt Top: The upper quilt layer, which forms the overall design.

Pieced Block: Small pieces of fabric in various shapes sewn together to form a larger design.

Sashing Strips: A strip of fabric sewn between the blocks and between rows of blocks.

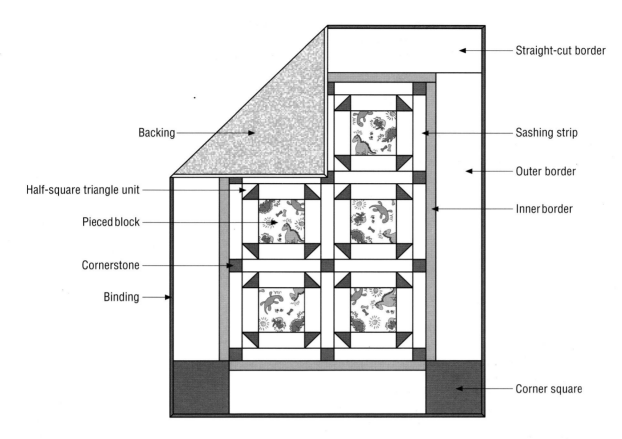

Straight-cut border

Backing

Sashing strip

Outer border

Half-square triangle unit

Inner border

Pieced block

Cornerstone

Binding

Corner square

Supplies

You will need a few basic supplies to make the quilts in this book:

100% cotton fabric
100% cotton thread for stitching
Cotton, rayon, or transparent monofilament thread for machine quilting
Sewing machine in good working order, with a walking foot or darning foot for machine quilting
Rotary-cutting equipment, including:
   rotary cutter
   cutting mat
   6" x 24" ruler
   12" x 12" ruler for squaring up blocks
   6" x 6" Omnigrid ruler for cutting the blocks on pages 54 and 56
Fine, thin pins
Fabric scissors
Seam ripper
Marking pencil
Safety pins or QuilTak basting gun

Selecting Fabrics

Buying fabric is my favorite part of the process. I love to see the new fabrics that are introduced each season. They seem to get more colorful and creative every year. When I see a print that I like, I buy it, even if I don't have a project in mind. Fabrics come and go quickly, so I buy them when I see them.

I generally start with one main print that catches my eye. I then search for a number of different fabrics that will go with the main print. Some patterns are easy, like "PS I Love You" (page 31), which requires only two contrasting fabrics. Others are a little more complicated, like "Junk Food Junkie" (page 22), which requires a main print and six coordinated fabrics.

I prefer 100% cotton fabric because it is easy to work with and launders beautifully. Many of the quilts I've made have been washed frequently, and they still look great. The colors in most of the cotton prints manufactured today hold up much better than they used to. My favorite fabrics are those from Hoffman of California and Alexander Henry. Each year, they introduce a fabulous array of colorful, whimsical prints that are perfect for the quilts I make.

I know many of you are going to see a fabric in one of the quilts in this book and wish you could find it. Unfortunately, you probably won't be able to find a lot of them. Between the time the quilts are made and the book is published, many fabrics will have come and gone. But don't let that stop you. There will be something just as bright and colorful available at your local quilt shop or fabric store.

When selecting fabrics, consider the following:
- Combine pure colors (primary colors) with other pure colors.
- Combine tints (soft pastels) with other tints.
- Vary the scale or busyness of the prints. Too much of the same thing can be boring.
- Look for solid-looking fabrics in addition to plain solids. These fabrics have a subtle texture that adds interest.

Don't be afraid to mix prints. I combine plaids, stripes, and dots with reckless abandon. My motto is "the busier, the better." I use prints in ways that force you to explore the surface to find the pattern. There are times when something soft and subtle is needed, and I can do that too, but it takes a bit more effort for me.

The Mickey Mouse faces in "Bright Mickeys" (page 24) were cut from boxer shorts I found in the Disney mail-order catalog. They even glow in the dark. I ordered several pairs in the extra-large size. After washing the shorts and undoing all the seams, I carefully planned my cutting so I could get as many motifs as possible from each pair. Because I was trying to get a balance of green, blue, red, and yellow motifs, I needed three pairs of shorts to make the twelve squares for the quilt.

If a print you like doesn't fit into a 6" square, don't get discouraged. It's easy to make adjustments to accommodate the fabric. Make the square larger or smaller and then adjust the other components in the quilt accordingly. For example, in "Frolicking Frogs" (page 30), the directions call for 6½" squares. The strips for the rectangles surrounding the squares are cut 6½" long. If your motifs fit better into a 5" finished square, then cut the squares 5½" and cut the strips for the rectangles 5½" long. Don't be afraid to change the sizes of the pieces. But don't forget to adjust the sizes of the other components, such as sashing strips, borders, and corner squares.

Cutting motifs for center squares from large-scale prints can present some problems. If the motifs are close together, you may be able to cut strips across the fabric width and then crosscut the strip into squares. If the motifs are farther apart and you don't want as much of the background in your squares, you will need to "fussy-cut" the motifs. I had to fussy-cut the squares from the fabrics used in "Java Beans" (page 28) and "Extinction is Forever" (page 30). Otherwise, I would not have been able to feature certain motifs as I did.

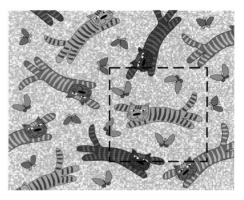

Cutting specific designs from fabric requires extra yardage. Plan your cuts carefully.

Preparing Fabrics

Fabrics are washed before they are allowed into my sewing room. This way, I don't have to stop and think about whether a piece of fabric on my shelf has been washed or not. It's also handy when I'm working late at night—I can just pull something from my shelf and use it. I prewash fabrics in warm water, without detergent, then tumble dry and iron them.

Yardage Requirements

The yardage requirements for the quilts in this book are based on at least 42" of usable width after prewashing. Several quilts actually require 42½"-long strips. If your fabric is narrower, you will need additional yardage so you can cut additional strips.

Rotary Cutting

Directions are for rotary cutting all pieces, and all measurements include ¼"-wide seam allowances.
1. Fold the fabric and match the selvages, aligning the crosswise and lengthwise grains as much as possible. Place the folded edge closest to you on the cutting mat.

2. Align a square ruler along the folded edge of the fabric. Then place a long, straight ruler to the left of the square, just covering the uneven raw edges of the fabric. Remove the square ruler and cut along the right edge of the ruler, rolling the rotary cutter away from you. Discard this strip. (Reverse this procedure if you are left-handed.)

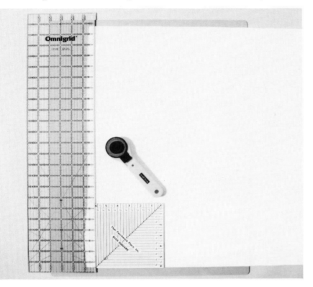

3. To cut strips, align the required measurement on the ruler with the newly cut edge of the fabric. For example, to cut a 2½"-wide strip, place the 2½" mark of the ruler on the edge of the fabric. A 2½"-wide strip, with a ¼"-wide seam allowance on each long edge (for a total of ½"), will finish to 2" wide.

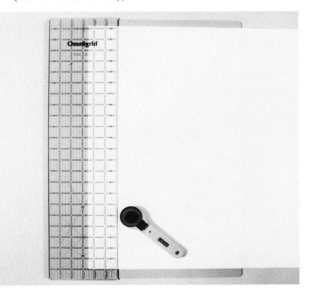

4. To cut squares and rectangles, cut strips in the required widths. Remove the selvage ends of the strip. Align the required measurement on the ruler with the left edge of the strip and cut a square or rectangle. Continue cutting until you have the number of pieces required.

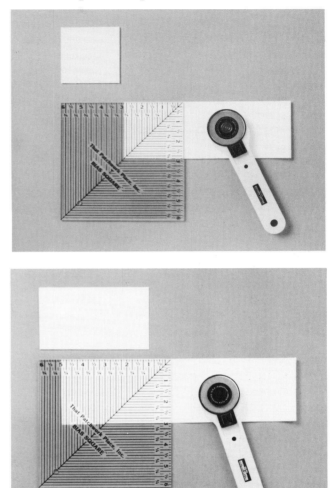

5. For some quilts, you will cut strips, sew them together in strip sets, then cut segments from the strip sets. First, trim the ends of the strip set to square it up. Align the required measurement on the ruler with the left edge of the strip set; cut the specified number of segments.

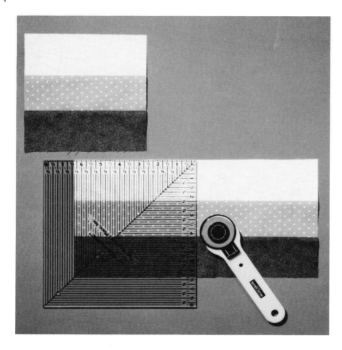

Piecing

All the blocks in this book are simple to make. The most important thing to remember is to maintain a consistent ¼"-wide seam allowance throughout your piecing. Otherwise, your block will not be the desired finished size. If that happens, the size of everything else in the quilt is affected—alternate blocks, sashing, and borders. Measurements for all components of the quilt are based on blocks that finish to the desired size plus ¼" all around for seams.

Creating an Accurate Seam Guide

Take the time to establish an exact ¼"-wide seam guide on your machine. Some sewing machines have a special quilting foot. With these, you can use the edge of the presser foot to guide the edge of the fabric for a perfect ¼"-wide seam.

If you don't have such a foot, create a seam guide with masking tape so it will be easy to stitch a ¼"-wide seam.

1. Place a ruler or piece of graph paper with four squares to the inch under your presser foot.
2. Gently lower the needle onto the first ¼" line from the right edge of the ruler or paper. Place several layers of masking tape or a piece of moleskin (available in drugstores) along the right edge of the ruler or paper, in front of the needle. Test your new guide to make sure your seams are ¼" wide; if not, readjust your seam guide.

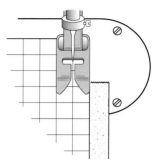

Piecing Half-Square Triangle Units

Four quilts in this book—"All-American Athlete" (page 18), "Flying High" (page 25), "Bears in a Wrench" (page 25), and "Frosty and Friends" (page 27) —require half-square triangle units. Use the following method to make these units.

1. Cut squares the size given in the quilt directions. Draw a diagonal line from corner to corner on the wrong side of the lightest fabric.

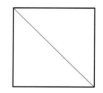

2. Place the square with the drawn line on top of a square of the contrasting fabric, right sides together. Sew ¼" away from the drawn line on both sides.

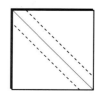

3. Cut on the drawn line. Open the unit and press the seams toward the darker fabric. Each pair of squares yields 2 half-square triangle units.

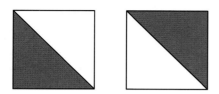

Pinning

Take the time to pin pieces together when assembling the blocks and the quilt top. On most machines, there is a tendency for the pieces to shift slightly as they are fed under the presser foot. A few carefully placed pins will keep this shifting to a minimum. Don't risk the possibility of unaligned seams or mismatched corners and points just to save a few minutes. *Pin!*

Pressing

I use a steam iron on a cotton setting to press all seams. Since all my fabrics are prewashed and ironed, I don't worry about pieces shrinking from the heat or steam of the iron. Press each seam after stitching and before adding other pieces.

1. Press the stitches flat along a seam line before pressing the seams to one side. This relaxes the thread and smooths out any puckers.

2. Working from the right side, press the seam toward the darker fabric. Be careful not to stretch the pieces out of shape as you press.

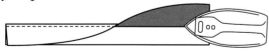

Pressing arrows are provided in several piecing and assembly diagrams, where the direction in which you press is important. Following these diagrams will help in constructing the blocks and assembling the quilt top.

Assembling the Quilt Top

When you have made all the blocks and cut all the remaining pieces, it's time to put them together to make the quilt top.

1. Following the quilt plan provided with each quilt, arrange the blocks.
2. Join the blocks in horizontal rows. Press the seams in opposite directions from row to row so opposing seams will butt against each other when you join the rows. Some quilts have specific directions for pressing the seams between blocks.

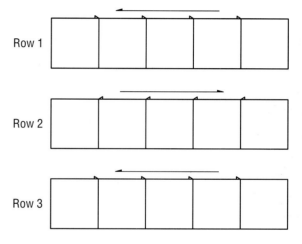

3. Join the rows, making sure to match the seams between the blocks.

For quilts with sashing strips and cornerstones, follow the quilt plan to arrange the blocks, sashing strips, and cornerstones. Join the blocks and sashing strips in horizontal rows; press the seams toward the sashing strips. Join the sashing strips and cornerstones in horizontal rows; press the seams toward the sashing strips. Join the rows, making sure to match the seams.

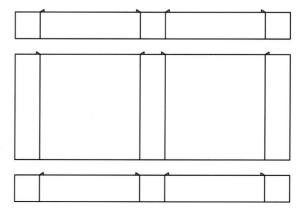

Finishing the Quilt

Adding Borders

For the simple quilts in this book, I prefer borders with straight-cut corners, and I generally repeat the main fabric in the border. This makes the decision about what fabric to use in the border an easy one. Border strips are usually cut across the width of the fabric. When these strips aren't long enough for the sides of a quilt, I piece the border strips and trim them to the required lengths. If you prefer unpieced borders, you will need to purchase extra fabric to cut full-length strips from the lengthwise grain. Three of the quilts have border strips cut from the lengthwise grain; additional yardage is provided to do this.

Sixteen of the quilts in this book have corner squares in the borders. This is an economical use of fabric since you can use shorter border strips. It's also a place to add another spot of color. If you prefer not to use corner squares, simply measure and cut border strips as instructed on page 11 for borders with straight-cut corners. You may need extra fabric to do this, so check your measurements.

It's important to measure and cut border strips to fit your quilt. Cutting strips and simply sewing them directly to the quilt top without measuring often results in a quilt with wavy borders. The edges of a quilt can be slightly longer than the distance through the center due to stretching during construction. Sometimes, each edge is a different length.

Specific measurements are provided for cutting the border strips for each quilt. These measurements are based on blocks sewn with accurate ¼"-wide seam allowances. Measure your blocks to be sure they are the correct size. To be safe, wait until the blocks are sewn together before cutting the border strips. Then measure your quilt top to determine the correct border lengths.

TIP

If you are working with a directional print, position the borders so the designs all face the center of the quilt. See "Tractors and Movers and Haulers, Oh My!" (page 29). All the wheels face toward the center.

A Word of Warning

If you accidentally cut a border strip too short, don't despair. With a bit of creativity, you can always make it work. I did just that in "Frosty and Friends" (page 27). I cut the side borders too short—way too short—and didn't have any more fabric. With no quilt shop open at two o'clock in the morning, I had to figure out something else. I experimented with adding different-sized strips and pretty soon had the answer. I cut red strips the width of the green cornerstones,

then cut snowman border strips so the red strips would line up with the green cornerstones—the perfect solution—but wait. I miscut the border strips again! That's why there is an additional green strip at each end of the borders. See, we all make mistakes. It turned out not to be such a bad mistake after all. The border on Frosty and Friends is much more exciting than if I had cut straight pieces.

Borders with Straight-Cut Corners

1. Measure the length of the quilt top through the center. Cut 2 border strips to that measurement, piecing strips as necessary. Mark the center of the quilt edges and the border strips.

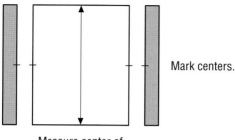

Mark centers.

Measure center of quilt, top to bottom.

2. Pin the borders to the sides of the quilt top, matching the center marks and ends and easing as necessary. Sew the borders in place. Press the seams toward the border.
3. Measure the width of the quilt top through the center, including the side borders just added. Cut border strips to that measurement, piecing strips as necessary. Mark, pin, and sew the borders in place as described for the side borders. Press the seams toward the border.

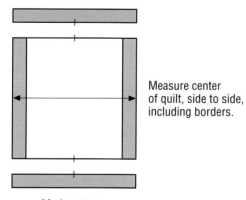

Measure center of quilt, side to side, including borders.

Mark centers.

Borders with Corner Squares

1. Measure the width and length of the quilt top through the center. Cut border strips to those measurements, piecing strips as necessary. Mark the center of the quilt edges and the border strips. Pin the side borders to opposite side edges of the quilt, matching the centers and ends and easing as necessary. Sew them in place. Press the seams toward the borders.
2. Cut corner squares or piece them as required. Sew a corner square to each end of the remaining border strips; press the seams toward the border strip. Pin the borders to the top and bottom edges, matching the centers, seams, and ends and easing as necessary. Sew them in place. Press the seams toward the border.

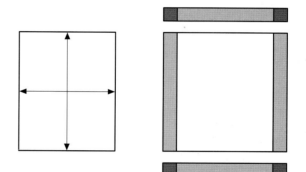

Backing

Cut the backing larger than the quilt top. This allows for any shifting of the layers that may occur while quilting and for the slight shrinkage that occurs when layers are quilted. Yardage requirements for backings are based on cutting the backing 4" longer and 4" wider than the quilt top. For example, cut a 46" x 46" backing for a quilt that measures 42" x 42". Since the standard width of cotton fabric is about 42", one length of fabric is not enough for a backing of this size; you will need two lengths.

The preferred method for piecing the backing is to cut one length in half and sew each half to opposite sides of a second length as shown. Trim the excess fabric and save the leftovers for other projects.

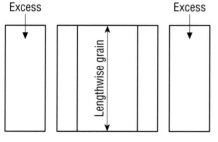

Lengthwise Backing

Some quilt plans direct you to piece the backing crosswise. When you do this, the seams will lie *across* the back of the quilt rather than lengthwise.

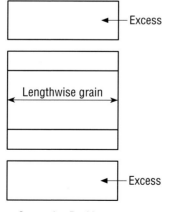

Crosswise Backing

Backing Options

There are several ways I use what I have on hand to make a backing the required size.
- I often piece the backing from leftover fabric. To do this, determine the required backing size and cut leftover fabrics into strips or squares. Sew them together randomly or in an interesting pattern, until you achieve the required size.

- If a piece of backing is only 2" to 5" shorter than required, I add a strip of fabric along one side or through the middle to make the backing the required size. This is also a good place to use leftover fabric from the front of the quilt. If you don't have one piece long enough, sew several pieces together to make the required length.

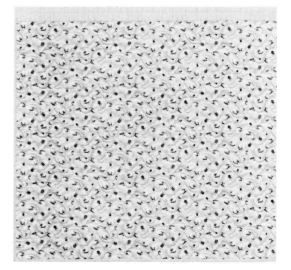

Making the Quilt Sandwich

The quilt sandwich is made up of the quilt top, batting, and backing. A thin, low-loft batting works well for either hand or machine quilting. My favorite batting is Soft Touch cotton batting by Fairfield. It is easy to handle when layering and a dream to quilt on. Warm & Natural is also easy to work with and does not need to be quilted as closely.

1. Unroll the batting and let it relax overnight before you layer your quilt. Cut the backing and batting 4" longer and 4" wider than the quilt top.
2. Place the backing, wrong side up, on a large table. Use masking tape or large binder clamps to anchor the backing to the table. Make sure the backing is flat and wrinkle-free, but be careful not to stretch it out of shape.
3. Place the batting on top of the backing, smoothing out all wrinkles.
4. Center the pressed quilt top, right side up, on top of the batting. Smooth out any wrinkles. Make sure the quilt-top edges are parallel to the backing edges.
5. Baste with safety pins or a QuilTak basting gun (available in most quilt shops). Place pins 4" to 6" apart, away from the area you intend to quilt. Sewing machines and safety pins do not get along!

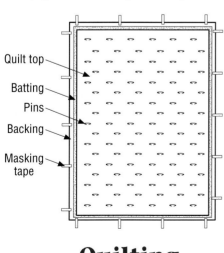

Quilt top
Batting
Pins
Backing
Masking tape

Quilting

All of my quilts are machine quilted because I don't have the time to hand quilt. I admire anyone who has the patience and the time to do it. I'm sure the babies for whom I make these quilts don't want to receive them as graduation gifts, so I take the easy way out.

Most of the quilts in this book are quilted with a combination of straight-line and free-motion quilting. I've even begun to play with some of the fancy stitches on my sewing machine. I used a double needle and a decorative stitch to quilt "Choo-Choo" (page 19) and "Frolicking Frogs" (page 30).

I use Mettler Silk Finish cotton (no. 50), Madiera Rayon (no. 40), or transparent monofilament thread for machine quilting. Finding a thread color to blend with all the prints can be difficult, but red seems to work with most of the primary-colored quilts. The variegated rayon threads also work well for multicolored quilt tops. If I can't decide on a thread color or don't want the thread to show at all, I use transparent monofilament thread.

Straight-Line Quilting

You will need a walking foot to help feed the quilt layers through the machine without shifting or puckering. I also use a walking foot when using decorative stitches. The Pfaff sewing machine has a built-in walking foot that I love. Other machines require a separate attachment.

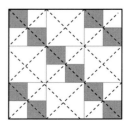

Walking foot

Use straight-line quilting to stitch straight lines, to outline-quilt, and to quilt "in-the-ditch."

Diagonal Straight Lines

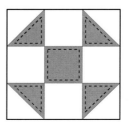

Outline Quilt

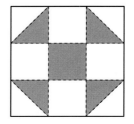

Quilt in-the-Ditch

Free-Motion Quilting

You will need a darning foot and the ability to drop or cover the feed dogs on your sewing machine. With free-motion quilting, you do not turn the fabric under the needle, but instead guide the fabric in the direction of the design. This technique requires some practice. I recommend that you practice for several hours before starting on a quilt.

Use free-motion quilting to outline-quilt a motif in the fabric or to create scribbles, stippling, and many other designs.

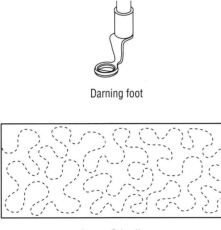

Darning foot

Large Stippling

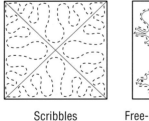

Scribbles   Free-Motion Outline Quilt

Tacking a Quilt by Machine

There is another way to secure the layers—you can tie or tack the quilt. If you look closely at "Hearts and Hands" (page 18), you'll see little circles all over the quilt. These circles were used to "tack" the layers together. This is similar to tying a quilt with yarn.

I chose a decorative stitch on my machine and selected the "single stitch" option. Then I stitched the circles randomly all over the quilt. The amount of tacking depends on the batting you use. For a batting that needs to be closely quilted, such as Soft Touch, I stitched a circle every 2" to 3". If you are using a batting like Warm & Natural, which only needs to be stitched every 8" to 10", you can make your tacks farther apart.

> ### TIP
>
> See Maurine Noble's book, Machine Quilting Made Easy, *for some quick and simple methods for tying or tacking a quilt by machine, plus many other machine-quilting tips.*

Binding

I prefer a double-fold, straight-cut binding. I use a double-fold, bias binding only when I want to change the direction of a print for the binding, such as placing a stripe on the diagonal. See "I Love Cats" (page 20) and "Bright Mickeys" (page 24) for examples.

To cut double-fold, straight-grain binding strips:

Cut the required number of 2¼"-wide strips across the width of the fabric. You will need enough strips to go around the perimeter of the quilt plus 10" for seams and the corners in a mitered fold.

To cut double-fold, bias binding strips:

1. Fold the fabric for the binding as shown. Pay careful attention to the location of the lettered corners.

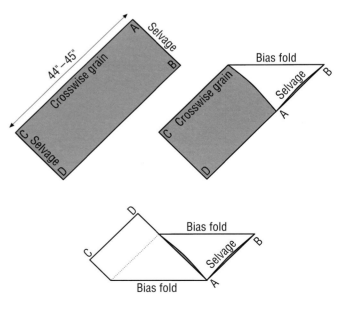

2. Cut strips 2¼" wide, cutting perpendicular to the folds as shown.

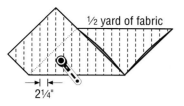

To attach the binding:
1. Trim the batting and backing even with the edges of the quilt top.
2. Join binding strips, right sides together, to make one long piece of binding. Press the seams open.

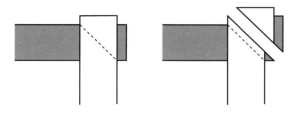

Joining Bias-Cut Strips

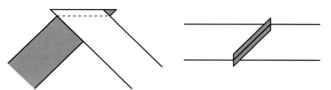

Joining Straight-Cut Strips

3. Fold the binding in half, wrong sides together; press.
4. Leaving the first 10" of binding unsewn, stitch the binding in place, using a ¼"-wide seam allowance. Stop stitching ¼" from the corner of the quilt and backstitch once. Clip the thread.

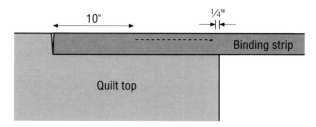

5. Turn the quilt so you will be stitching down the next side. Fold the binding up, away from the quilt. Then fold the binding back down onto itself, keeping the fold parallel with the edge of the quilt top. Begin stitching at the edge, backstitching to secure.

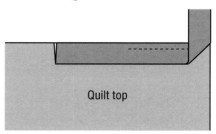

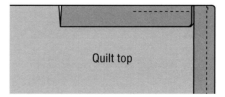

6. Repeat steps 4 and 5 on the remaining edges and corners of the quilt. When you are within 10" of the starting point, remove the quilt from the sewing machine and lay the unsewn section on a flat surface. Fold the unsewn binding ends back on themselves so they just meet in the middle over the unsewn area of the quilt top. Finger-press or pin both bindings to mark this junction.

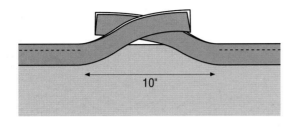

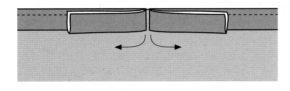

7. Unfold both sides of the bindings and match the centers of the pressed **X**s. Sew across the intersection as when sewing the binding strips together. Trim the excess fabric and press the seam open. Finish stitching the binding to the quilt edge.

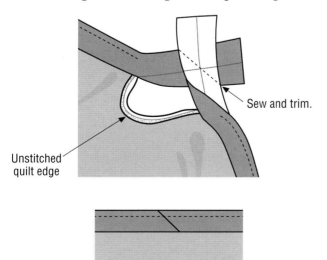

8. Fold the binding over the raw edges to the back. Blindstitch in place, with the folded edge covering the row of machine stitching. A miter will form at each corner. Blindstitch the mitered corners in place.

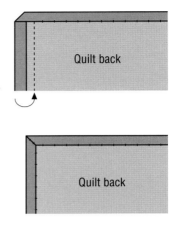

Adding a Label

Don't forget to make a label for your quilt. Include your name, city and state, the date, and the recipient if it is a gift. You can machine embroider the information, or write it with a permanent marking pen. Sew the label to the back of the finished quilt.

Gallery of Quilts

Lunchtime! by Ursula Reikes, 1996,
Redmond, Washington, 56½" x 72½".
What goes better with frogs than bugs?
Two simple blocks, Four Patch and
Snowball, combine to make this
appealing luncheon for the frogs.
Directions begin on page 71.

All-American Athlete by Ursula Reikes, 1996, Redmond, Washington, 44½" x 58½". A little bit of everything in this print will inspire your favorite athlete. The Kitty Corner block gives you plenty of room to spotlight a special print. Made for grandson Gino. Directions begin on page 62.

Hearts and Hands by Ursula Reikes, 1996, Redmond, Washington, 58¼" x 67". A coordinated collection of Patrick Lose prints were used for this easy Five-Stripe block. Made for Kelsey Jordan Early, to keep at Doodle's house. Directions begin on page 34.

Choo-Choo by Ursula Reikes, 1996, Redmond, Washington, 52½" x 65½". Coxey's Camp, an obscure traditional block, is the perfect companion for the trains in this print. It looks like the trains just tumbled from the tracks and are waiting to be put back. The railroad tracks were quilted with a double needle. Directions begin on page 48.

Tumbling Teddies by Ursula Reikes, 1996, Redmond, Washington, 40½" x 40½". Dreamy little teddy bears floating on pink and blue pastel skies make a perfect nap-time cover for your favorite little one. Directions begin on page 52.

I Love Cats by Ursula Reikes, 1996, Redmond, Washington, 46½" x 62½". The Chinese Coins pattern is the quickest and easiest way to use a collection of theme fabrics. This quilt features twenty-nine different cat prints and one mouse print. Directions begin on page 38.

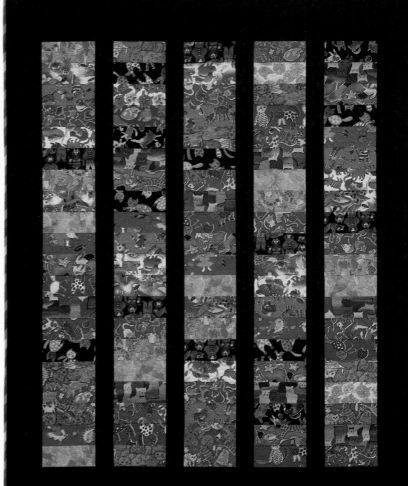

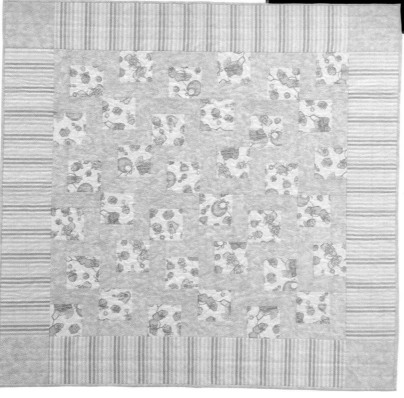

Bundle of Joy by Ursula Reikes, 1996, Redmond, Washington, 48½" x 48½". Patience Corners is the perfect block for a baby quilt, because you need so much patience with children. A double needle was used to stipple-quilt the center. Made for Josepha Rose Cisakowski, the adorable baby on the cover of this book. Directions begin on page 42.

Laura's Quilt by Ursula Reikes, 1994, Redmond, Washington, 50½" x 50¼". The wonderful animal print fabric called out for a unique design. With just a tiny bit of math, it was easy to showcase each of the animals in the print. Made for Laura Voss. This is Laura's wall quilt. Parents Diane and Charlie say she has to name all the animals before she will leave her crib in the morning. Directions begin on page 77.

BZZZZZZ! by Ursula Reikes, 1996, Redmond, Washington, 40½" x 40½". A block from the International Signal Flags, the W block goes together quickly. Only three fabrics are needed for this eye-catching pattern. Directions begin on page 46.

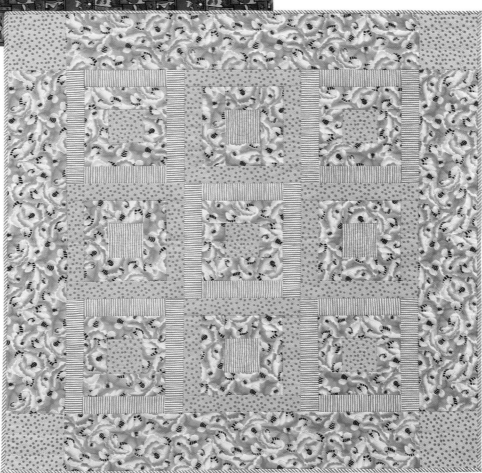

Junk Food Junkie by Ursula Reikes, 1996, Redmond, Washington, 45½" x 56". This is a wonderful quilt for a college student's taste buds. A variation of the traditional Log Cabin, this block has logs added to only two sides. Made for Elizabeth Aracic. Directions begin on page 74.

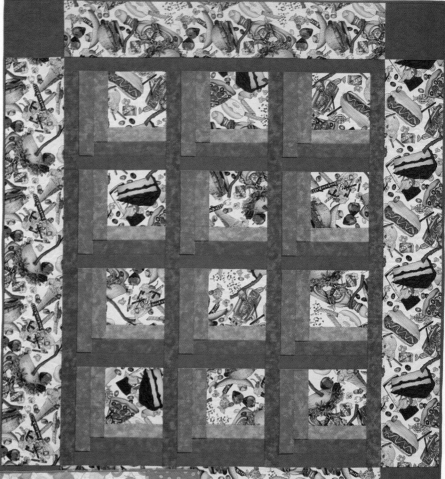

Spinning Balloons by Ursula Reikes, 1996, Redmond, Washington, 48" x 48". Quick and easy strip piecing make this block a snap to construct. No templates are needed. Made for Anya Charlie Rauchle. Directions begin on page 54.

Prism Houndstooth by Ursula Reikes, 1996, Redmond, Washington, 48" x 59". This block is a variation of the Windmill block (previous page). The basic construction is the same; only the orientation of the squares is different. Made for Alex Amma Rauchle. Directions begin on page 56.

Fabricaholic by Ursula Reikes, 1997, Redmond, Washington, 48" x 59". This color version of the Houndstooth block features prints from the Story Cloth line "The Fabric Sale," designed by Mary Lou Weidman for In The Beginning Fabrics. Made for Deborah Aracic, a true fabricaholic friend.

Will Work for Fabric by Ursula Reikes, 1997, Redmond, Washington, 38½" x 48½". How many of us feel as if we do just work for fabric, as we watch our fabric stash grow larger every year? The Bright Hopes block features more of Mary Lou Weidman's colorful prints from the Story Cloth line "The Fabric Sale" by In The Beginning fabrics. Directions begin on page 50.

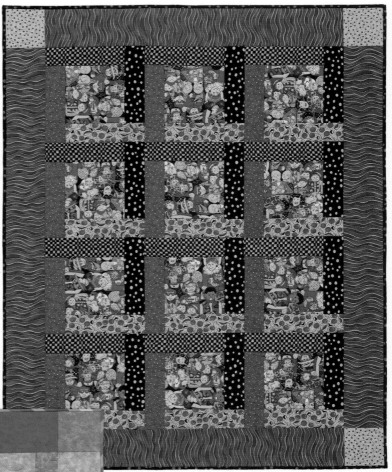

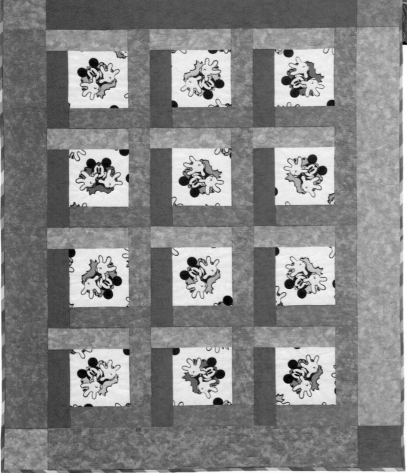

Bright Mickeys by Ursula Reikes, 1996, Redmond, Washington, 38½" x 48½". The Bright Hopes block is also the perfect showcase for Mickey Mouse. These Mickeys, which were cut from boxer shorts ordered through the Disney catalog, even glow in the dark. Made for William Nelson Voss.

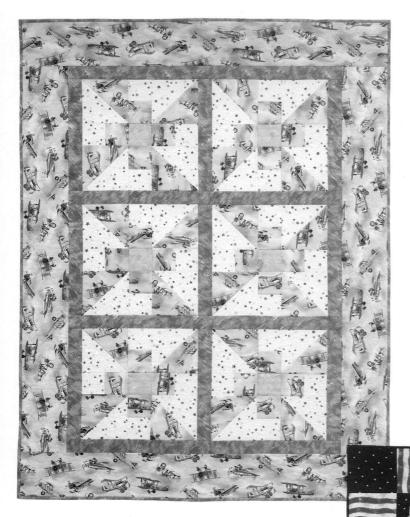

Flying High *by Ursula Reikes, 1996, Redmond, Washington, 40" x 54". The airplane fabric and the Propeller block make a perfect combination. Made for Julian Christian Larsen. Directions begin on page 60.*

Bears in a Wrench *by Ursula Reikes, 1996, Redmond, Washington, 40" x 54". The Monkey Wrench and the Propeller blocks (above) are made with the same units; only the orientation of the large half-square triangle units is changed.*

Ladybug, Ladybug, Fly Away Home
by Ursula Reikes, 1996, Redmond, Washington, 40½" x 46½". Like stars floating across the sky, ladybugs float from block to block in this X-quisite pattern, which is also called Skewed Stars. Sometimes you see them, sometimes you don't. It all depends on where you look. Directions begin on page 58.

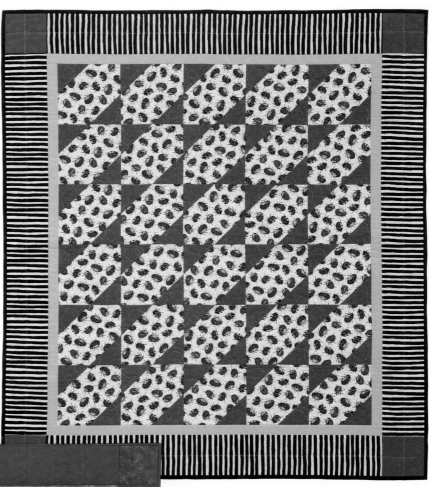

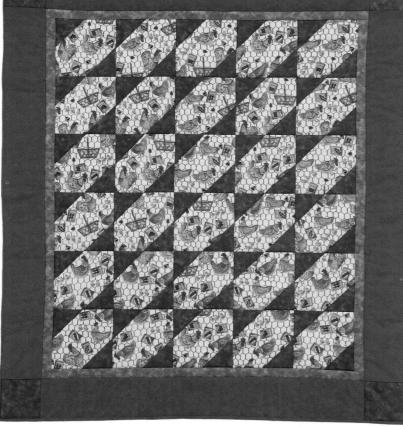

Cody's Prize-Winning Flock *by Marion Shelton, 1996, Mill Creek, Washington, 40½" x 46½". When I suggested a "chicken" quilt, Marion immediately thought of her great-nephew Cody Payne, who is carrying on the family tradition of leadership in Future Farmers of America. Collection of Cody Payne.*

Frosty and Friends *by Ursula Reikes, 1996, Redmond, Washington, 42" x 55½". Frosty and his friends are surrounded by snow and seasonal colors in this Pinwheel block. The unusual border is the result of a cutting error (see page 10). Directions begin on page 64.*

Ladybug Picnic *by Donna Lever, 1996, Maple Valley, Washington, 42" x 55½". Donna likes ladybugs, so she decided to feature them in this striking version of the Pinwheel block. She made this special quilt for Mia Kathryn Creighton of Grayslake, Illinois.*

Dinosaurs Love Veggies by Ursula Reikes, 1996, Redmond, Washington, 44" x 54". The Scotch Quilt block isn't seen often, but it's a playful block with a lot of options for placing fabrics. Directions begin on page 68.

Java Beans by Ursula Reikes, 1996, Redmond, Washington, 35½" x 49½". This version of the Scotch Quilt block features a coffee motif for a coffee-loving friend, Carol Doak.

Tractors and Movers and Haulers, Oh My! *by Ursula Reikes, 1996, Redmond, Washington, 39½" x 52". The Off-Center Log Cabin blocks create a network of roads for the trucks in this print. Made for Nathaniel Christian Willert. Directions begin on page 66.*

Provence *by Ursula Reikes, 1996, Redmond, Washington, 46½" x 57½". Fabric from the Nancy J. Martin Room Mates™ collection inspired this French Country quilt. The logs in the Off-Center Log Cabin block were adjusted to accommodate the width of the print. As a rule, the wide logs should be twice as wide as the narrow logs, but you can change the rules to suit your needs.*

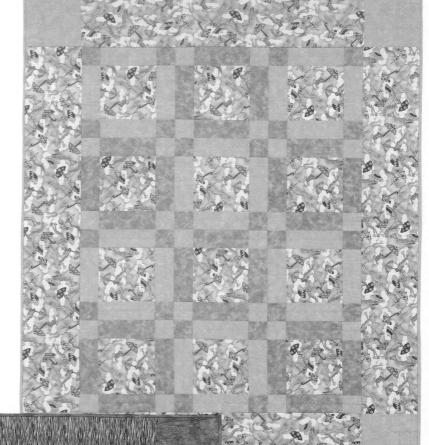

Frolicking Frogs by Ursula Reikes, 1996, Redmond, Washington, 42½" x 52½". Playful frogs leap across the quilt, jumping from block to block. The Plaid Squares block is super simple and goes together in a flash. Made for David Cornish Jacobsen, son of our cats' favorite veterinarian. Directions begin on page 40.

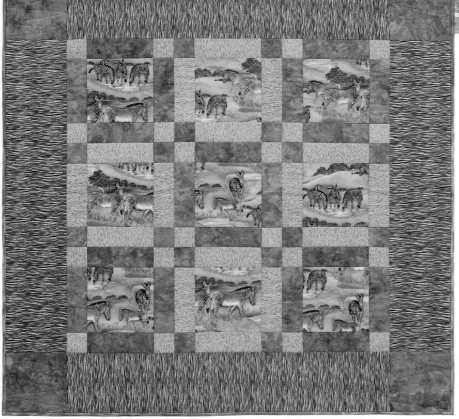

Extinction Is Forever by Ursula Reikes, 1996, Redmond, Washington, 42½" x 42½". The center of the Plaid Squares block is a perfect place to use large theme prints. Make a quilt featuring your passions.

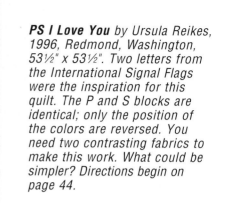

PS I Love You *by Ursula Reikes, 1996, Redmond, Washington, 53½" x 53½". Two letters from the International Signal Flags were the inspiration for this quilt. The P and S blocks are identical; only the position of the colors are reversed. You need two contrasting fabrics to make this work. What could be simpler? Directions begin on page 44.*

E is for Elephant *by Ursula Reikes, 1997, Redmond, Washington, 57½" x 57½". Although the contrast between the fabrics is not as great in this version of the P and S blocks, that doesn't stop the fun. The bright, colorful letters and whimsical elephants provide an eyeful for a toddler just learning her ABCs. Made for Laura Voss (her snuggle quilt).*

Stars and Stripes by Ursula Reikes, 1996, Redmond, Washington, 43" x 43". This is the simplest of all pinwheels to make. With strip piecing, you can make the whole quilt in an afternoon. My patriotic version uses four red-and-white prints, but it works just as well with only two contrasting fabrics. Directions begin on page 36.

A Plethora of Pansies by Ursula Reikes, 1997, Redmond, Washington, 43" x 43". This bold version of the Edna's Pinwheel block features just two contrasting fabrics, plus a coordinating inner border and binding. With this quick pattern, it's easy to make something special for a special friend. Made for Trish Carey.

The Quilts

Look through the gallery and find a quilt that appeals to you. Consider the size of the quilt and the complexity of the pattern. If you don't have a lot of time, "Stars and Stripes" (opposite) or "Frolicking Frogs" (page 30) are good choices. Both of these quilts go together quickly. If you have more time and want a bit more of a challenge, try "Laura's Quilt" (page 21), which has a free-form block or "Frosty and Friends" (page 27).

If you see a quilt you like, but you'd like to make it smaller or larger, that's easy. Simply increase or reduce the number of blocks or change the size of the borders. Read through the directions and look at the illustrations of the quilt you want to make. You'll quickly see how the pieces are cut and assembled. Adjust the yardage requirements up or down and make notes on how many pieces you'll need for your project.

Your fabric choices may also influence your decision on which quilt to make. For example, if you want to use a fabric that has a large motif, one of the patterns with a 6" square would be appropriate. Patterns like "Bright Mickeys" (page 24) or "Dinosaurs Love Veggies" (page 28) are perfect for featuring large designs. On the other hand, if you want to use a variety of fabrics with smaller designs, consider patterns like "Hearts and Hands" (page 18) or "Stars and Stripes" (opposite).

The most important part of the process is to have fun. Once you achieve success with one quilt, you'll want to make quilts for everyone. Remember, these quilts aren't just for babies.

Hearts and Hands

Color Photo: page 18
Quilt Size: 58¼" x 67"
Finished Block Size: 8¾" x 8¾"

Five Stripe Block
Make 30.

Materials 44"-wide fabric		Cutting Cut all strips across the fabric width.			
		First Cut		**Second Cut**	
Fabric	Yardage	No. of Strips	Strip Size	No. of Pieces	Piece Size
Fabric A	⅝ yd.	8	2¼" x 42"		
Fabric B	⅝ yd.	8	2¼" x 42"		
Fabric C	⅝ yd.	8	2¼" x 42"		
Fabric D	⅝ yd.	8	2¼" x 42"		
Fabric E	⅝ yd.	8	2¼" x 42"		
Border	1⅛ yds.	5	7½" x 42"		
Corner squares	¼ yd.	1	7½" x 42"	4	7½" x 7½"
Backing	3½ yds. (pieced crosswise)				
Binding	½ yd.	7	2¼" x 42"		

Quilt Top Assembly

1. Make 8 strip sets as shown. Cut a total of 30 segments, each 9¼"* wide, from the strip sets.

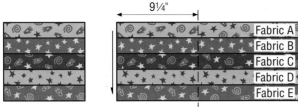

Cut 30.

Make 8 strip sets.

*Measure the width of the strip set before cutting the segments. If it is not 9¼" wide, cut your strip sets into segments, using the actual width of your strip set. For example, if your strip sets are only 9" wide, then cut 9"-wide segments. The end result must be a square.

2. Arrange the blocks as shown.

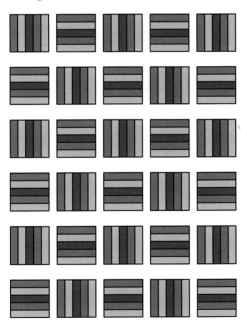

3. Join the blocks in horizontal rows. Press the seams in opposite directions from row to row. Join the rows, making sure to match the seams between the blocks.

Quilt Finishing

Refer to "Finishing the Quilt" on pages 10–16.

1. Join the 5 border strips end to end to make one long continuous strip. From the long strip, cut 2 strips, each 53" long, for the side borders, and 2 strips, each 44¼" long, for top and bottom borders.
2. Sew the border strips to the side edges of the quilt top first. Add a corner square to each end of the remaining border strips and stitch them to the top and bottom edges.

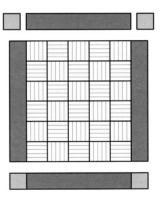

3. Layer the quilt top with batting and backing; baste. Quilt as desired.
4. Bind the edges. Label your quilt.

Stars and Stripes

Color Photo: page 32
Quilt Size: 43" x 43"
Finished Block Size: 5" x 5"

Edna's Pinwheel Block A
Make 20.

Edna's Pinwheel Block B
Make 16.

Materials	Cutting				
44"-wide fabric	*Cut all strips across the fabric width.*				
		First Cut		Second Cut	
Fabric	*Yardage*	*No. of Strips*	*Strip Size*	*No. of Pieces*	*Piece Size*
Fabric A	⅓ yd.	3	3" x 42"		
Fabric B	⅝ yd.	6	3" x 42"		
Fabric C	⅓ yd.	3	3" x 42"		
Inner border	¼ yd.				
(sides)		2	1¾" x 30½"		
(top/bottom)		2	1¾" x 33"		
Outer border	¾ yd.	4	5½" x 33"		
Corner squares	¼ yd.	1	5½" x 42"	4	5½" x 5½"
Backing	2¾ yds.*				
Binding	⅜ yd.	5	2¼" x 42"		

*Or purchase only 1⅜ yds. and add leftovers from the front to make a creative backing. See page 12.

Quilt Top Assembly

1. Make 3 each of Strip Sets #1 and #2 as shown. Press the seams toward the darker fabric. From Strip Set #1, cut a total of 20 segments, each 5½" wide. From Strip Set #2, cut a total of 16 segments, each 5½" wide.

Cut 20.

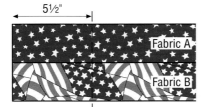

Strip Set #1
Make 3.

Cut 16.

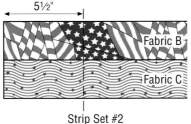

Strip Set #2
Make 3.

2. Arrange the blocks as shown, rotating them as needed to form pinwheels.

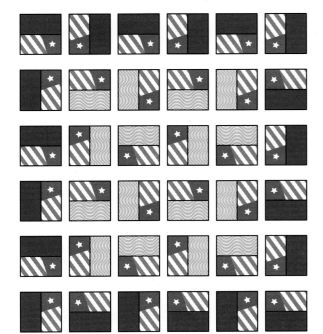

3. Join the blocks in horizontal rows. Press the seams in opposite directions from row to row. Join the rows, making sure to match the seams between the blocks.

Quilt Finishing

Refer to "Finishing the Quilt" on pages 10–16.
1. Sew the inner border strips to the side edges of the quilt top first, then to the top and bottom.
2. Sew the outer border strips to the side edges of the quilt top first. Add a corner square to each end of the remaining outer border strips, then stitch them to the top and bottom edges.

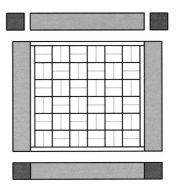

3. Layer the quilt top with batting and backing; baste. Quilt as desired.
4. Bind the edges. Label your quilt.

I Love Cats

Color Photo: page 20
Quilt Size: 46½" x 62½"

Materials		Cutting	
44"-wide fabric		*Cut all strips across the fabric width unless otherwise indicated.*	
Fabric	**Yardage**	**No. of Strips**	**Strip Size**
10 different prints	fat qtr. each (18" x 21")	3 (from each print)	3" x 21"
		From leftover fabric, cut 10 rectangles, each 3" x 6½".	
Sashing & Border (sashing)	1½ yds.*	4	2½" x 50½"
(sides)		2	4½" x 50½"
(top/bottom)		2	6½" x 46½"
Backing	2⅞ yds. (pieced crosswise)		
Binding	½ yd.	6	2¼" x 42"

*Cut strips from the lengthwise grain of the fabric.

This quilt is the perfect place to use a collection of fabrics or lots of leftovers from previous projects. I cut one strip from each of thirty different fabrics to make the quilt shown on page 20. The directions below are for making a similar quilt using only ten fat quarters and quick strip-piecing methods.

If you are using a collection of smaller scraps, simply cut 100 rectangles, each 2½" x 6½". Join 20 rectangles to make one long row. Make 5 rows. Follow the directions on page 39 to finish your quilt. You can easily adjust the size of this quilt by using more or fewer rectangles.

Quilt Top Assembly

1. Make 3 strip sets as shown, using 10 different 3" x 21" strips in each set. From the strip sets, cut a total of 9 segments, each 6½" wide.

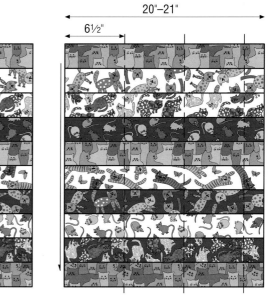

Cut 9.   Make 3 strip sets.

2. Join 2 segments to make one long row. Make 4 rows.

Join 2 segments.
Make 4.

3. To make the 5th row, join the 10 individual rectangles and add them to the remaining 6½"-wide segment.

4. Join the rows and sashing strips as shown. Press the seams toward the sashing strips.

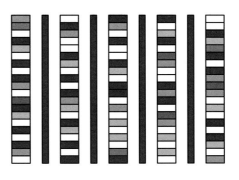

Quilt Finishing

Refer to "Finishing the Quilt" on pages 10–16.

1. Sew the 4½"-wide borders to the side edges of the quilt top first, then add the 6½"-wide borders to the top and bottom.

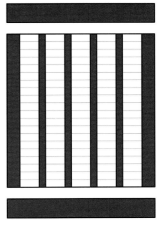

2. Layer the quilt top with batting and backing; baste. Quilt as desired.
3. Bind the edges. Label your quilt.

Join 10 rectangles and add to remaining pieced segment to make the 5th row.

Frolicking Frogs

Color Photo: page 30
Quilt Size: 42½" x 52½"
Finished Block Size: 10" x 10"

Plaid Squares Block A
Make 6.

Plaid Squares Block B
Make 6.

Materials		First Cut		Second Cut	
44"-wide fabric		**Cut all strips across the fabric width.**			
Fabric	*Yardage*	*No. of Strips*	*Strip Size*	*No. of Pieces*	*Piece Size*
Theme print	½ yd.	2	6½" x 42"		
Fabric A	⅝ yd.	4	2½" x 42"		
		1	6½" x 42"		
Fabric B	⅝ yd.	4	2½" x 42"		
		1	6½" x 42"		
Border	⅞ yd.				
(sides)		2	6½" x 40½"		
(top/bottom)		2	6½" x 30½"		
Corner squares	¼ yd.	1	6½" x 42"	4	6½" x 6½"
Backing	2¾ yds.* (pieced crosswise)				
Binding	⅜ yd.	5	2¼" x 42"		

*Or purchase only 1¾ yds. and add leftovers from the front to make a creative backing. See page 12.

Quilt Top Assembly

1. Make 1 each of Strip Sets #1, #2, #3, and #4. From each of Strip Sets #1 and #2, cut 12 segments, each 2½" wide. From each of Strip Sets #3 and #4, cut 6 segments, each 6½" wide.

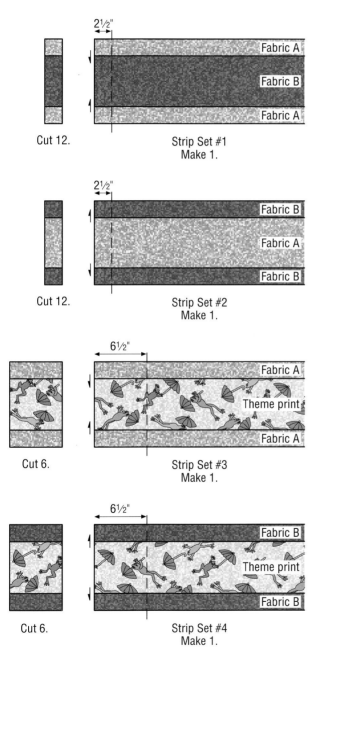

2½"

Cut 12.

Fabric A

Fabric B

Fabric A

Strip Set #1
Make 1.

2½"

Cut 12.

Fabric B

Fabric A

Fabric B

Strip Set #2
Make 1.

6½"

Cut 6.

Fabric A

Theme print

Fabric A

Strip Set #3
Make 1.

6½"

Cut 6.

Fabric B

Theme print

Fabric B

Strip Set #4
Make 1.

2. Make a total of 12 Plaid Square blocks as shown: 6 A blocks and 6 B blocks.

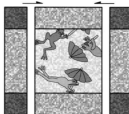 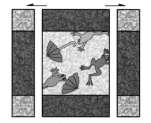

Block A
Make 6.

Block B
Make 6.

3. Arrange the blocks, alternating the A and B blocks as shown.

4. Join the blocks in horizontal rows. Press the seams in opposite directions from row to row. Join the rows, making sure to match the seams between the blocks.

Quilt Finishing

Refer to "Finishing the Quilt" on pages 10–16.

1. Sew the border strips to the side edges of the quilt top first. Add a corner square to each end of the remaining border strips, then stitch them to the top and bottom edges.

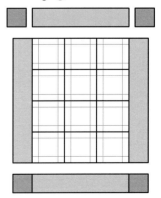

2. Layer the quilt top with batting and backing; baste. Quilt as desired.
3. Bind the edges. Label your quilt.

Bundle of Joy

Color Photo: page 20
Quilt Size: 48½" x 48½"
Finished Block Size: 12" x 12"

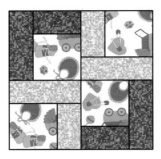

Patience Corners Block
Make 9.

Materials		Cutting			
44"-wide fabric		*Cut all strips across the fabric width.*			
		First Cut		**Second Cut**	
Fabric	**Yardage**	**No. of Strips**	**Strip Size**	**No. of Pieces**	**Piece Size**
Theme print	⅝ yd.	4	4½" x 42"		
Fabric A (corner square)	⅝ yd.	5 1	2½" x 42" 6½" x 13"	2	6½" x 6½"
Fabric B (corner square)	⅝ yd.	5 1	2½" x 42" 6½" x 13"	2	6½" x 6½"
Border	⅞ yd.	4	6½" x 36½"		
Backing	3 yds.*				
Binding	⅜ yd.	5	2¼" x 42"		

*Or purchase only 1½ yds. and add leftovers from the front to make a creative backing. See page 12.

Quilt Top Assembly

1. Make 2 each of Strip Sets #1 and #2 as shown. Cut a total of 18 segments, each 4½" wide, from Strip Set #1, and a total of 18 segments, each 4½" wide, from Strip Set #2.

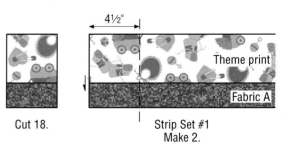

Cut 18.

4½"

Theme print

Fabric A

Strip Set #1
Make 2.

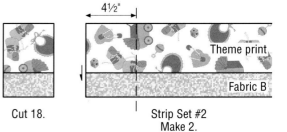

Cut 18.

4½"

Theme print

Fabric B

Strip Set #2
Make 2.

2. With the large square closest to you, place the units on top of a 2½"-wide strip to match the A or B fabric in the unit. Position the units next to each other without overlapping the edges. Stitch. Cut between the units, trimming away any excess fabric.

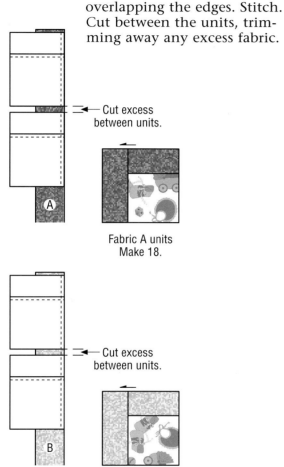

Fabric A units
Make 18.

Fabric B units
Make 18.

3. Make 9 Patience Corners blocks, each using 2 Fabric A units and 2 Fabric B units as shown.

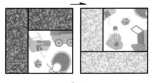
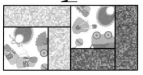

Make 9.

4. Arrange the blocks as shown.

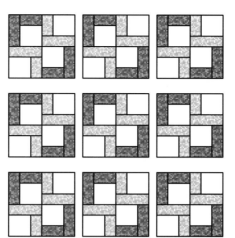

5. Join the blocks in horizontal rows. Press the seams in opposite directions from row to row. Join the rows, making sure to match the seams between the blocks.

Quilt Finishing

Refer to "Finishing the Quilt" on pages 10–16.

1. Sew the border strips to the side edges of the quilt top first. Add a Fabric A corner square to one end of each of the remaining border strips; add a Fabric B square to the other end. Attach the borders to the top and bottom edges, placing the matching corner squares in opposite diagonal corners.

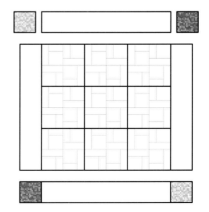

2. Layer the quilt top with batting and backing; baste. Quilt as desired.
3. Bind the edges. Label your quilt.

PS I Love You

Color Photo: page 31
Quilt Size: 53½" x 53½"
Finished Block Size: 9" x 9"

P Block
Make 13.

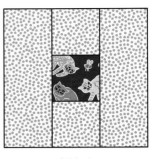

S Block
Make 12.

Materials 44"-wide fabric		Cutting *Cut all strips across the fabric width.*	
Fabric	**Yardage**	**No. of Strips**	**Strip Size**
Fabric A	1⅛ yds.	10	3½" x 42"
Fabric B	1 yd.	9	3½" x 42"
Inner border	¼ yd.	5	1½" x 42"
Outer border	⅔ yd.	6	3½" x 42"
Backing	3¼ yds.		
Binding	½ yd.	6	2¼" x 42"

Quilt Top Assembly

1. Make 1 each of Strip Sets #1 and #2. From each of the strip sets, cut 12 segments, each 3½" wide.

2. Since you can only cut 12 segments from a 42" long strip, you will need to make a 13th segment for the P blocks. From one of the Fabric A strips, cut 2 squares, each 3½" x 3½". From one of the Fabric B strips, cut 1 square, 3½" x 3½". Join the squares to make the 13th segment.

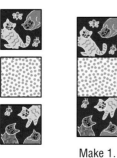

Make 1.

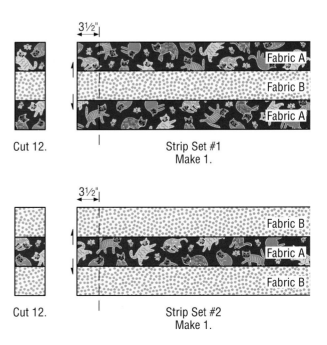

Cut 12.

3½"

Fabric A
Fabric B
Fabric A

Strip Set #1
Make 1.

Cut 12.

3½"

Fabric B
Fabric A
Fabric B

Strip Set #2
Make 1.

3. To make the P blocks, place the segments from Strip Set #1 on top of a 3½"-wide Fabric A strip. Place the segments next to each other without overlapping the edges. Stitch. Do not cut apart yet.

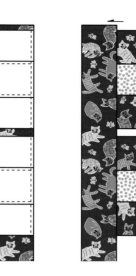

4. Turn the strip of sewn segments around and place the opposite side of the segments on top of another 3½"-wide Fabric A strip. Place the segments next to each other without overlapping the edges. Stitch.

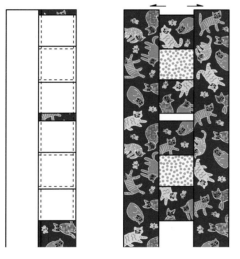

5. Lay the sewn unit on the cutting mat. Use a ruler and rotary cutter to cut between the units, trimming away any excess fabric between the units.

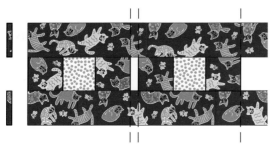

6. Repeat steps 3–5 to make the S Blocks, but this time use segments from Strip Set #2 and Fabric B strips.

7. Arrange the blocks, alternating P and S blocks in each row as shown. Rotate the blocks so the long seams are horizontal in the P blocks and vertical in the S blocks.

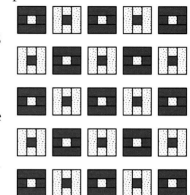

8. Join the blocks in horizontal rows. Press the seams toward the P blocks. Join the rows, making sure to match the seams between the blocks.

Quilt Finishing

Refer to "Finishing the Quilt" on pages 10–16.

1. Join the 5 inner border strips end to end to make one long strip. From the long strip, cut 2 strips, each 45½" long, for the side borders, and 2 strips, each 47½" long, for the top and bottom borders.
2. Sew the inner border strips to the side edges of the quilt top first, then to the top and bottom.
3. Join the 6 outer border strips end to end to make one long strip. From the long strip, cut 2 strips, each 47½" long, for the side borders, and 2 strips, each 53½" long, for the top and bottom borders.
4. Sew the outer border strips to the side edges first, then to the top and bottom.

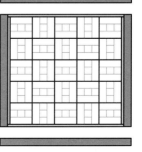

5. Layer the quilt top with batting and backing; baste. Quilt as desired.
6. Bind the edges. Label your quilt.

BZZZZZZ!

Color Photo: page 21
Quilt Size: 40½" x 40½"
Finished Block Size: 10" x 10"

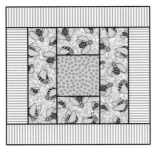

W Block 1
Make 5.

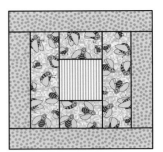

W Block 2
Make 4.

Materials 44"-wide fabric		Cutting Cut all strips across the fabric width.			
		First Cut		**Second Cut**	
Fabric	Yardage	No. of Strips	Strip Size	No. of Pieces	Piece Size
Theme print	½ yd.	6	2½" x 42"	4	2½" x 21"
Fabric A	½ yd.	1	3½" x 21"		
		5	2" x 42"		
Fabric B	½ yd.	1	3½" x 21"		
		4	2" x 42"		
Border	¾ yd.	4	5½" x 30½"		
Corner squares	¼ yd.	1	5½" x 42"	4	5½" x 5½"
Backing	1¼ yds.				
Binding	⅓ yd.	4	2¼" x 42"		

Quilt Top Assembly

1. Using the 21"-long strips, make 1 each of Strip Sets #1 and #2 as shown. From Strip Set #1, cut 4 segments, each 3½" wide. From Strip Set #2, cut 5 segments, each 3½" wide.

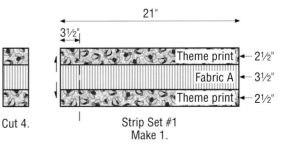

Cut 4. Strip Set #1 Make 1.

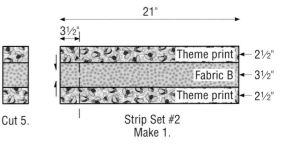

Cut 5. Strip Set #2 Make 1.

2. Using 42"-long strips, make 2 each of Strip Sets #3 and #4. From Strip Set #3, cut a total of 10 segments, each 7½" wide. From Strip Set #4, cut a total of 8 segments, each 7½" wide.

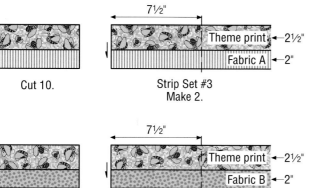

Cut 10.

Strip Set #3
Make 2.

Theme print ← 2½"
Fabric A ← 2"

Cut 8.

Strip Set #4
Make 2.

Theme print ← 2½"
Fabric B ← 2"

3. From the remaining 2"-wide strips, cut 10 segments, each 2" x 10½", from Fabric A, and 8 segments, each 2" x 10½", from Fabric B.

4. Assemble the segments as shown to make the W blocks in 2 different configurations. Press the seams away from the center of the block.

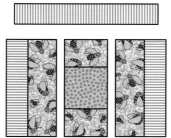

W Block 1
Make 5.

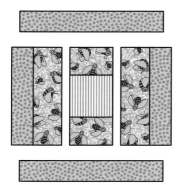

W Block 2
Make 4.

5. Arrange the blocks as shown, rotating them as necessary to create the pattern. Rotate the blocks so the longest seams are horizontal in the W2 blocks and vertical in the W1 blocks.

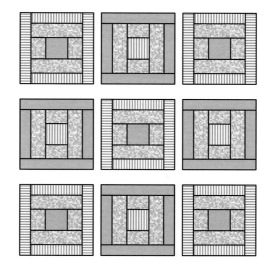

6. Join the blocks in horizontal rows. Press the seams in opposite directions from row to row. Join the rows, making sure to match the seams between the blocks.

Quilt Finishing

Refer to "Finishing the Quilt" on pages 10–16.

1. Sew the border strips to the side edges of the quilt top first. Add a corner square to each end of the remaining border strips, then stitch them to the top and bottom edges.

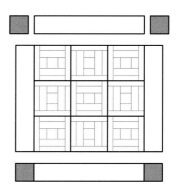

2. Layer the quilt top with batting and backing; baste. Quilt as desired.
3. Bind the edges. Label your quilt.

Choo-Choo

Color Photo: page 19
Quilt Size: 52½" x 65½"
Finished Block Size: 12" x 12"

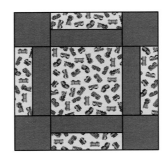

Coxey's Camp
Make 12.

Materials / Cutting

Fabric	Yardage	No. of Strips	Strip Size	No. of Pieces	Piece Size
Materials *44"-wide fabric*		**Cutting** *Cut all strips across the fabric width.*			
		First Cut		**Second Cut**	
Theme print	1 yd.	8	2" x 42"		
		2	6½" x 42"		
Background	1 yd.	8	2" x 42"		
		4	3½" x 42"	48	3½" x 3½"
Sashing/Inner border	⅝ yd.	1	12½" x 42"	16	1½" x 12½"
		5	1½" x 40½"		
Outer border	1⅛ yds.	5	6½" x 42"		
Corner squares	¼ yd.	1	6½" x 42"	4	6½" x 6½"
Backing	3¼ yds. (pieced crosswise)				
Binding	½ yd.	6	2¼" x 42"		

Quilt Top Assembly

1. Make 2 of Strip Set #1 and 4 of Strip Set #2 as shown. From Strip Set #1, cut a total of 12 segments, each 6½" wide. From Strip Set #2, cut a total of 24 segments, each 6½" wide.

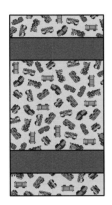

Cut 12.

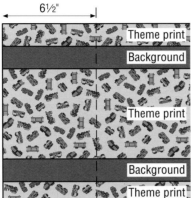

Strip Set #1
Make 2.

Theme print
Background
Theme print
Background
Theme print

6½"

Cut 24.

6½"

Background
Theme print

Strip Set #2
Make 4.

2. Make 12 Coxey's Camp blocks as shown.

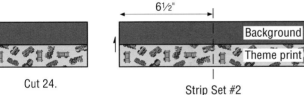

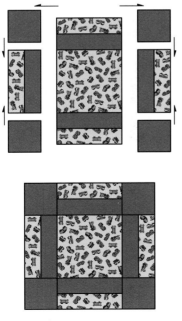

Make 12.

3. Arrange the blocks and sashing strips as shown.

4. Join the blocks and sashing strips in horizontal rows. Press the seams toward the sashing strips. Join the rows, adding the horizontal sashing strips between the rows and to the top and bottom edges.

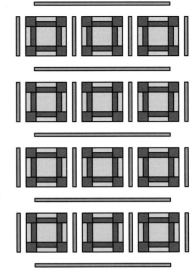

Quilt Finishing

Refer to "Finishing the Quilt" on pages 10–16.

1. Join 3 outer border strips end to end to make one long continuous strip. From the long strip, cut 2 strips, each 53½" long, for the side borders. Trim each of the remaining 2 outer border strips to 40½" for the top and bottom borders.

2. Sew the outer borders to the sides first. Add a corner square to each end of the remaining outer border strips and attach them to the top and bottom edges.

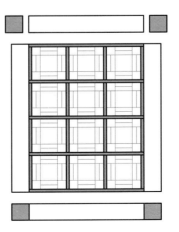

3. Layer the quilt top with batting and backing; baste. Quilt as desired.

4. Bind the edges. Label your quilt.

Will Work for Fabric

Color Photo: page 24
Quilt Size: 38½" x 48½"
Finished Block Size: 10" x 10"

Bright Hopes Block
Make 12.

Materials *44"-wide fabric*		Cutting *Cut all strips across the fabric width.*			
		First Cut		**Second Cut**	
Fabric	*Yardage*	*No. of Strips*	*Strip Size*	*No. of Pieces*	*Piece Size*
Theme print	½ yd.*	2	6½" x 42"	12	6½" x 6½"
Fabric A	⅜ yd.	3	2½" x 42"	12	2½" x 8½"
Fabric B	⅜ yd.	3	2½" x 42"	12	2½" x 8½"
Fabric C	⅜ yd.	3	2½" x 42"	12	2½" x 8½"
Fabric D	⅜ yd.	3	2½" x 42"	12	2½" x 8½"
Borders	⅝ yd.				
(sides)		2	4½" x 40½"		
(top/bottom)		2	4½" x 30½"		
Corner Squares	¼ yd.	1	4½" x 18"	4	4½" x 4½"
Backing	1½ yds.				
Binding	⅜ yd.	5	2¼" x 42"		

*You will need additional yardage if you want to center specific designs within each square.

Quilt Top Assembly

1. Sew a 2½" x 8½" Fabric A piece to the bottom of a theme print square as shown. Stitch from the corner of the square to the halfway point; stop and remove the unit from the machine. This is called a partial seam.

Stop stitching at halfway point.

2. Sew Fabric B, C, and D pieces to the remaining sides of the square in the order shown. Stitch from edge to edge. Press the seams away from the center square.

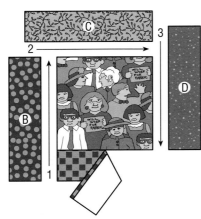

3. Sew the remainder of the partial seam to complete the block.

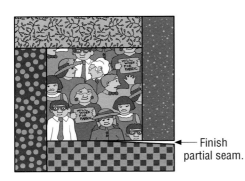

Finish partial seam.

4. Arrange the blocks as shown.

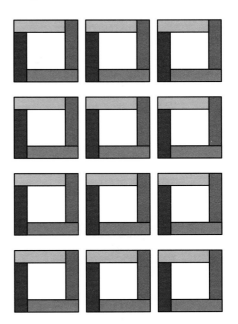

5. Join the blocks in horizontal rows. Press the seams in opposite directions from row to row. Join the rows, making sure to match the seams between the blocks.

Quilt Finishing

Refer to "Finishing the Quilt" on pages 10–16.
1. Sew the border strips to the side edges of the quilt top first. Add a corner square to each end of the remaining border strips, then stitch them to the top and bottom edges.

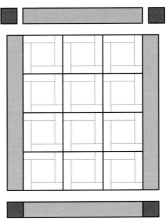

2. Layer the quilt top with batting and backing; baste. Quilt as desired.
3. Bind the edges. Label your quilt.

Tumbling Teddies

Color Photo: page 19
Quilt Size: 40½" x 40½"
Finished Block Size: 10" x 10"

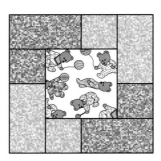

Square Illusion Block
Make 9.

Materials		Cutting			
44"-wide fabric		Cut all strips across the fabric width.			
		First Cut		**Second Cut**	
Fabric	Yardage	No. of Strips	Strip Size	No. of Pieces	Piece Size
Theme print	⅜ yd.*	2	5½" x 42"	9	5½" x 5½"
Fabric A	⅝ yd.	1	3" x 42"		
		1	3" x 14"		
		1	5½" x 42"		
		1	5½" x 42"	1	5½" x 14"
(corner squares)				2	5½" x 5½"
Fabric B	⅝ yd.	1	3" x 42"		
		1	3" x 14"		
		1	5½" x 42"		
		1	5½" x 42"	1	5½" x 14"
(corner squares)				2	5½" x 5½"
Borders	¾ yd.	4	5½" x 30½"		
Backing	1¼ yds.				
Binding	⅓ yd.	4	2¼" x 42"		

*You will need additional yardage if you want to center specific designs within each square.

Quilt Top Assembly

1. Make Strip Sets #1 and #2 in 2 different lengths as shown. From Strip Set #1, cut a total of 18 segments, each 3" wide. From Strip Set #2, cut a total of 18 segments, each 3" wide.

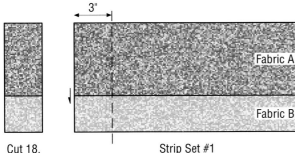

Cut 18.

Strip Set #1
Make one 42"-long strip set.
Make one 14"-long strip set.

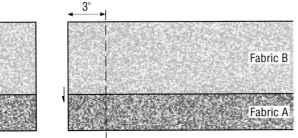

Cut 18.

Strip Set #2
Make one 42"-long strip set.
Make one 14"-long strip set.

2. Sew a segment from Strip Set #1 to the bottom of a theme print square as shown. Stitch from the corner of the square to the halfway point; stop and remove the unit from the machine. This is called a partial seam.

3. Sew 3 segments to the remaining sides of the square, alternating segments from Strip Set #1 and Strip Set #2 as shown. Stitch from edge to edge. Press the seams away from the center square.

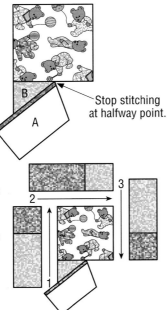

Stop stitching at halfway point.

4. Sew the remainder of the partial seam to complete the block.

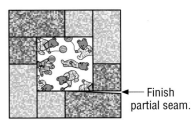

Finish partial seam.

5. Arrange the squares as shown.

6. Join the blocks in horizontal rows. Press the seams in opposite directions from row to row. Join the rows, making sure to match the seams between the blocks.

Quilt Finishing

Refer to "Finishing the Quilt" on pages 10–16.

1. Sew the border strips to the side edges of the quilt top first. Add a Fabric A corner square to one end of each of the remaining border strips, and a Fabric B corner square to the other end. Stitch these border strips to the top and bottom edges, placing matching corner squares in opposite diagonal corners.

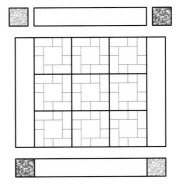

2. Layer the quilt top with batting and backing; baste. Quilt as desired.
3. Bind the edges. Label your quilt.

Spinning Balloons

Color Photo: page 22
Quilt Size: 48" x 48"
Finished Block Size: 5½" x 5½"

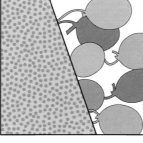

Windmill Block Unit A
Make 20.

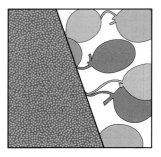

Windmill Block Unit B
Make 16.

Materials		First Cut		Second Cut	
44"-wide fabric		Cut all strips across the fabric width.			
Fabric	Yardage	No. of Strips	Strip Size	No. of Pieces	Piece Size
Theme print	1⅛ yds.	8	4¼" x 42"		
Fabric A	⅝ yd.	4	4¼" x 42"		
Fabric B	⅝ yd.	4	4¼" x 42"		
Inner border	⅓ yd.				
(sides)		2	2" x 33½"		
(top/bottom)		2	2" x 36½"		
Outer border	⅞ yd.	4	6¼" x 36½"		
Corner squares	¼ yd.	1	6¼" x 42"	4	6¼" x 6¼"
Backing	3 yds.*				
Binding	⅜ yd.	5	2¼" x 42"		

*Or purchase only 1½ yds. and add leftovers from the front to make a creative backing. See page 12.

Quilt Top Assembly

You will need a 6"-square ruler to cut the 6" squares for this quilt. The ruler should have inch marks, 1"–6", on opposite sides of the square.

1. Make 4 each of Strip Sets #1 and #2. Position a 6"-square ruler on the seam of the strip set, aligning the 4" mark on one side and the 2" mark on the opposite side with the seam line. Cut around all 4 sides of the ruler. Be careful not to shift the ruler as you cut. From Strip Set #1, cut a total of 20 squares. From Strip Set #2, cut a total of 16 squares.

Cut 20.

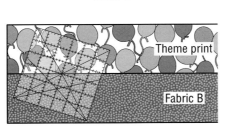

Strip Set #1
Make 4.

Cut 16.

Strip Set #2
Make 4.

2. Arrange the blocks as shown, rotating them as needed to form the pinwheels.

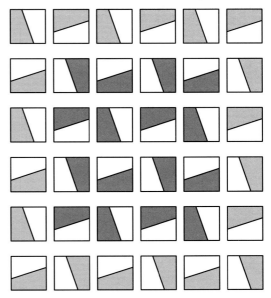

3. Join the blocks in horizontal rows. Press the seams in opposite directions from row to row. Join the rows, making sure to match the seams between the blocks.

Quilt Finishing

Refer to "Finishing the Quilt" on pages 10–16.

1. Sew the inner border strips to the side edges of the quilt top first, then to the top and bottom.
2. Sew the outer border strips to the side edges first. Add a corner square to each end of the remaining outer border strips, then stitch them to the top and bottom edges.

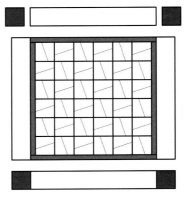

3. Layer the quilt top with batting and backing; baste. Quilt as desired.
4. Bind the edges. Label your quilt.

Prism Houndstooth

Color Photo: page 23
Quilt Size: 48" x 59"
Finished Block Size: 11" x 11"

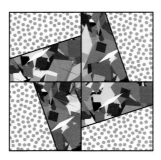

Houndstooth Block
Make 12.

Materials / Cutting

Fabric	Yardage	No. of Strips	Strip Size
Materials *44"-wide fabric*		**Cutting** *Cut all strips across the fabric width.*	
Fabric A	1⅛ yds.	8	4¼" x 42"
Fabric B	1⅛ yds.	8	4¼" x 42"
Inner border	⅜ yd.	5	2" x 42"
Outer border	1 yd.	5	6¼" x 42"
Backing	3 yds. (pieced crosswise)		
Binding	½ yd.	6	2¼" x 42"

Quilt Top Assembly

1. Using the 4¼"-wide Fabric A and B strips, follow the directions on page 55, step 1, to construct the strip sets and cut the 6" squares. Cut a total of 48 squares.

Cut 48.

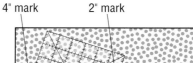
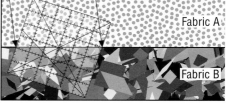

4" mark   2" mark

Fabric A

Fabric B

Make 8.

2. Make 12 Houndstooth blocks.

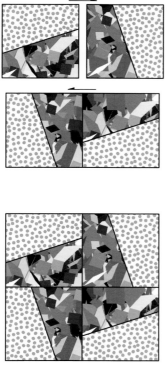

Make 12.

3. Arrange the blocks as shown.

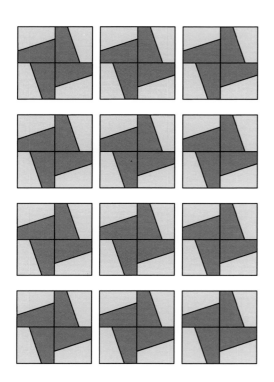

4. Join the blocks in horizontal rows. Press the seams in opposite directions from row to row. Join the rows, making sure to match the seams between the blocks.

Quilt Finishing

Refer to "Finishing the Quilt" on pages 10–16.

1. Join 3 inner border strips end to end to make one long continuous strip. From the long strip, cut 2 strips, each 44½" long, for the side borders. Trim the remaining 2 inner border strips to 36½" for the top and bottom borders.
2. Sew the inner border strips to the side edges of the quilt top first, then to the top and bottom.
3. Join the 5 outer border strips end to end to make one long continuous strip. From the long strip, cut 2 strips, each 47½" long, for the side borders, and 2 strips, each 48" long, for the top and bottom borders.
4. Sew the outer border strips to the side edges first, then to the top and bottom.

5. Layer the quilt top with batting and backing; baste. Quilt as desired.
6. Bind the edges. Label your quilt.

Ladybug, Ladybug, Fly Away Home

Color Photo: page 26
Quilt Size: 40½" x 46½"
Finished Block Size: 6" x 6"

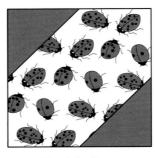

X-quisite Block
Make 30.

Materials 44"-wide fabric		Cutting *Cut all strips across the fabric width.*			
		First Cut		**Second Cut**	
Fabric	Yardage	No. of Strips	Strip Size	No. of Pieces	Piece Size
Theme print	1 yd.	5	6½" x 42"	30	6½" x 6½"
Star points	⅝ yd.	5	3½" x 42"	60	3½" x 3½"
Inner border	¼ yd.				
(sides)		2	1½" x 36½"		
(top/bottom)		2	1½" x 32½"		
Outer border	⅝ yd.				
(sides)		2	4½" x 38½"		
(top/bottom)		2	4½" x 32½"		
Corner squares	¼ yd.	1	4½" x 18"	4	4½" x 4½"
Backing	1½ yds.*				
Binding	⅜ yd.	5	2¼" x 42"		

*If the backing fabric is not wide enough for the quilt, add leftovers from the front to make a creative backing. See page 12.

Quilt Top Assembly

1. Draw a diagonal line from corner to corner on the wrong side of each 3½" star-point square.

2. Place a 3½" square on the upper left corner of a 6½" theme print square, right sides together, as shown. Stitch on the line. Trim, leaving a ¼"-wide seam allowance. Press the triangle toward the corner. Repeat with another 3½" square on the opposite diagonal corner.

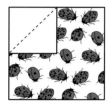

Stitch.   Trim.

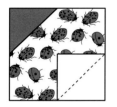

Stitch.   Trim.

Make 30.

3. Arrange the blocks as shown.

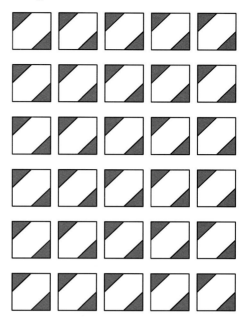

4. Join the blocks in horizontal rows. Press the seams in opposite directions from row to row. Join the rows, making sure to match the seams between the blocks.

Quilt Finishing

Refer to "Finishing the Quilt" on pages 10–16.

1. Sew the inner border strips to the side edges of the quilt top first, then to the top and bottom.
2. Sew the outer border strips to the side edges first. Add a corner square to each end of the remaining outer border strips, then stitch them to the top and bottom edges.

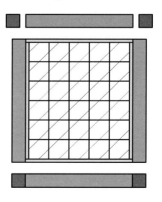

3. Layer the quilt top with batting and backing; baste. Quilt as desired.
4. Bind the edges. Label your quilt.

Flying High

Color Photo: page 25
(See also "Bears in a Wrench"
on page 25.)
Quilt Size: 40" x 54"
Finished Block Size: 12½" x 12½"

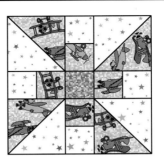

Propeller Block
Make 6.

OR

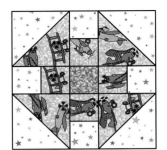

Monkey Wrench Block
Make 6.

Materials		Cutting			
44"-wide fabric		Cut all strips across the fabric width.			
		First Cut		Second Cut	
Fabric	Yardage	No. of Strips	Strip Size	No. of Pieces	Piece Size
Theme print	⅝ yd.	2	3" x 42"		
		2	5⅞" x 42"	12	5⅞" x 5⅞"
Background	⅝ yd.	2	3" x 42"		
		2	5⅞" x 42"	12	5⅞" x 5⅞"
Center squares	⅛ yd.	1	3" x 18"	6	3" x 3"
Sashing/Inner border	½ yd.	3	2" x 42"	9	2" x 13"
		4	2" x 30"		
Outer border	⅞ yd.	5	5½" x 42"		
Backing	1⅝ yds.				
Binding	⅜ yd.	5	2¼" x 42"		

Quilt Top Assembly

1. Make 24 half-square triangle units as shown on page 8, using the 5⅞" squares cut from the theme print and background fabric.

Make 24.

Note

The Propeller block and the Monkey Wrench block are made with the same units. See step 3 to make the block you prefer.

2. Make 2 strip sets as shown. From the strip sets, cut a total of 24 segments, each 3" wide.

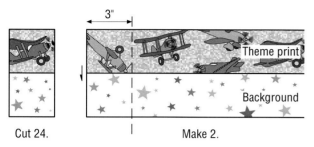

Cut 24. Make 2.

3. Make 6 Propeller blocks *or* Monkey Wrench blocks as shown.

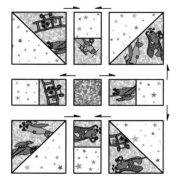

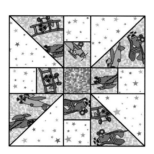

Propeller Block
Make 6.

OR

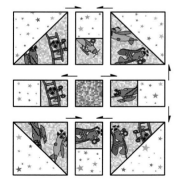

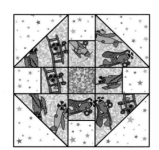

Monkey Wrench Block
Make 6.

4. Arrange the blocks and sashing strips as shown.

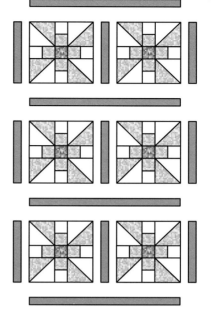

5. Join the blocks in horizontal rows, adding the 13" sashing strips between the blocks and at each end. Press the seams toward the sashing strips. Join the rows of blocks, adding a horizontal sashing strip between each row and to the top and bottom edges.

Quilt Finishing

Refer to "Finishing the Quilt" on pages 10–16.

1. Join 3 outer border strips end to end to make one long continuous strip. From the long strip, cut 2 strips, each 44" long, for the side borders. Trim each of the remaining 2 border strips to 40" for the top and bottom borders.

2. Sew the border strips to the side edges first, then to the top and bottom.

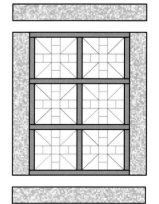

3. Layer the quilt top with batting and backing; baste. Quilt as desired.

4. Bind the edges. Label your quilt.

All-American Athlete

Color Photo: page 18
Quilt Size: 44½" x 58½"
Finished Block Size: 12" x 12"

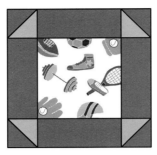

Kitty Corner Block
Make 6.

Materials 44"-wide fabric		Cutting Cut all strips across the fabric width.			
		First Cut		**Second Cut**	
Fabric	*Yardage*	*No. of Strips*	*Strip Size*	*No. of Pieces*	*Piece Size*
Theme print	½ yd.	2	7½" x 42"	6	7½" x 7½"
Fabric A	⅝ yd.	2	7½" x 42"	24	3" x 7½"
		1	3⅜" x 42"	12	3⅜" x 3⅜"
Fabric B	⅛ yd.	1	3⅜" x 42"	12	3⅜" x 3⅜"
Sashing/Inner border	⅝ yd.				
(sashing)		3	2½" x 42"	7	2½" x 12½"
(top border)		1	2½" x 26½"		
(sides)		2	2½" x 40½"		
(bottom border)		1	2½" x 26½"		
Cornerstones	⅛ yd.	1	2½" x 15"	6	2½" x 2½"
Middle border	¼ yd.	5	1½" x 42"		
Outer border	1 yd.	5	6½" x 42"		
Corner squares	¼ yd.	1	7½" x 42"	4	7½" x 7½"
Backing	2¾ yds.* (pieced crosswise)				
Binding	½ yd.	6	2¼" x 42"		

*Or purchase only 1¾ yds. and add leftovers from the front to make a creative backing. See page 12.

Quilt Top Assembly

1. Make 24 half-square triangle units as shown on page 8, using the 3⅜" squares cut from Fabrics A and B.

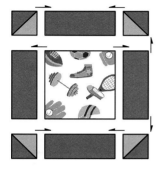

Make 24.

2. Make 6 Kitty Corner blocks as shown.

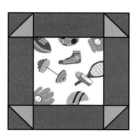

Make 6.

3. Arrange the blocks, sashing strips, and cornerstones as shown.

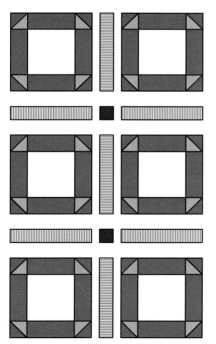

4. Join the blocks in horizontal rows, adding the 12½"-long sashing strips between the blocks. Press the seams toward the sashing strips.
5. Join the sashing strips and cornerstones in horizontal rows. Press the seams toward the sashing strips.
6. Join the rows of blocks and sashing.

Quilt Finishing

Refer to "Finishing the Quilt" on pages 10–16.

1. Sew the inner border strips to the side edges of the quilt top first. Add a cornerstone to each end of the remaining inner border strips and attach them to the top and bottom edges.
2. Join 3 middle border strips end to end to make one long continuous strip. From the long strip, cut 2 strips, each 44½" long, for the side borders. Trim each of the remaining 2 middle border strips to 30½" long for the top and bottom. Repeat with the outer border.
3. Sew the middle border strips to the corresponding outer border strips.

Make 2 side borders.
Make 2 top and bottom botders.

4. Sew the pieced borders to the sides first. Add a corner square to each end of the remaining pieced border strips and stitch them to the top and bottom edges.

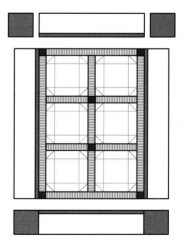

5. Layer the quilt top with batting and backing; baste. Quilt as desired.
6. Bind the edges. Label your quilt.

Frosty and Friends

Color Photo: page 27
Quilt Size: 42" x 55½"
Finished Block Size: 12" x 12"

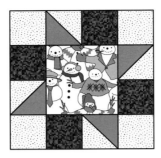

Pinwheel Block
Make 6.

Materials		Cutting			
44"-wide fabric		*Cut all strips across the fabric width.*			
		First Cut		Second Cut	
Fabric	Yardage	No. of Strips	Strip Size	No. of Pieces	Piece Size
Theme print	¼ yd.*	1	6½" x 42"	6	6½" x 6½"
Background	⅞ yd.	2	3⅞" x 42"	12	3⅞" x 3⅞"
		2	3½" x 42"	24	3½" x 3½"
(sashing)		6	2" x 42"	17	2" x 12½"
Green	⅜ yd.	2	3½" x 42"	24	3½" x 3½"
(cornerstones)		1	2" x 42"	12	2" x 2"
(outer border)		2	1" x 42"	8	1" x 6½"
Red	⅝ yd.	2	3⅞" x 42"	12	3⅞" x 3⅞"
(inner border/sides)		2	1" x 42½"**		
(inner border/top/bottom)		2	1" x 30"		
(corner squares)		1	6½" x 42"	4	6½" x 6½"
(outer border)				6	2" x 6½"
Outer border	⅞ yd.	1	14" x 42"	4	6½" x 14"
				2	6½" x 12½"
		2	6½" x 42"	4	6½" x 14"
Backing	2⅝ yds.				
	(pieced crosswise)				
Binding	⅜ yd.	5	2¼" x 42"		

*You will need additional yardage if you want to center specific designs within each square.
**If your fabric is not 42½", cut 1 more strip and piece the side strips.

Quilt Top Assembly

1. Make 24 half-square triangle units as shown on page 8, using the 3⅞" squares cut from the background and red fabrics.

Make 24.

2. Make 6 Pinwheel blocks as shown.

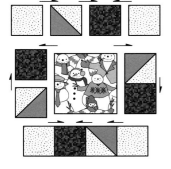

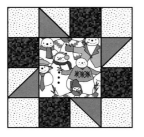
Make 6.

3. Arrange the blocks, sashing strips, and cornerstones as shown below.

4. Sew the blocks together in horizontal rows, adding the 12½"-long sashing strips between the blocks and at each end. Press the seams toward the sashing strips.
5. Sew the sashing strips and cornerstones together; press the seams toward the sashing strips.
6. Join the rows of blocks and sashing.

Quilt Finishing

Refer to "Finishing the Quilt" on pages 10–16.

1. Sew the inner border strips to the side edges of the quilt top first, then to the top and bottom.
2. Join the outer border pieces as shown below to make the top and bottom and side borders. If you are using a directional print, orient the pieces accordingly.

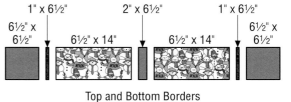
Top and Bottom Borders
Make 2.

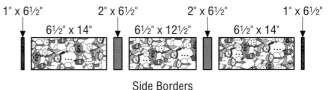
Side Borders
Make 2.

3. Sew the pieced borders to the side edges first, then to the top and bottom.

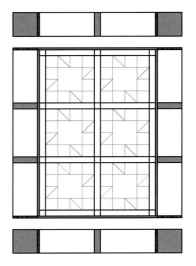

4. Layer the quilt top with batting and backing; baste. Quilt as desired.
5. Bind the edges. Label your quilt.

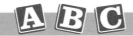

Tractors and Movers and Haulers, Oh My!

Color Photo: page 29
Quilt Size: 39½" x 52"
Finished Block Size: 12½" x 12½"

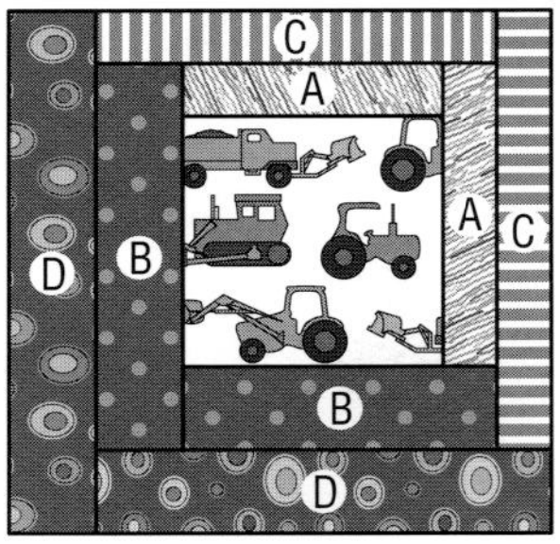

Off-Center Log Cabin Block
Make 6.

Materials 44"-wide fabric		**Cutting** Cut all strips across the fabric width.			
		First Cut		**Second Cut**	
Fabric	*Yardage*	*No. of Strips*	*Strip Size*	*No. of Pieces*	*Piece Size*
Theme print	¼ yd.*	1	6½" x 42"		
Fabric A	¼ yd.	3	1¾" x 42"		
Fabric B	¼ yd.	3	2½" x 42"		
Fabric C	¼ yd.	4	1¾" x 42"		
Fabric D	⅜ yd.	4	2½" x 42"		
Inner border	¼ yd.				
(sides)		2	1½" x 38"		
(top/bottom)		2	1½" x 27½"		
Outer border	⅞ yd.				
(sides)		2	6½" x 40"		
(top/bottom)		2	6½" x 27½"		
Corner squares	¼ yd.	1	6½" x 42"	4	6½" x 6½"
Backing	1⅝ yds.				
Binding	⅜ yd.	5	2¼" x 42"		

*You will need additional yardage if you want to center specific designs within each square.

Quilt Top Assembly

1. To quick-piece the center square and the first log, make 1 strip set as shown. From the strip set, cut 6 segments, each 6½" wide.

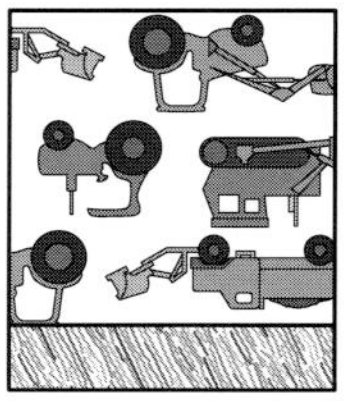

Cut 6.

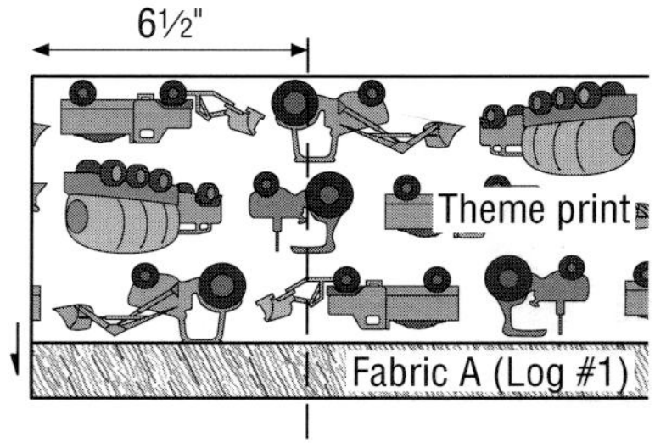

Make 1.

Note

If you cut the 6½" squares individually to center specific designs, you will not be able to do step 1. Instead, place the squares on top of Log #1, right sides together. Position the squares next to each other without overlapping the edges. Stitch. Cut between the units, trimming any excess fabric. Press the seams away from the center square.

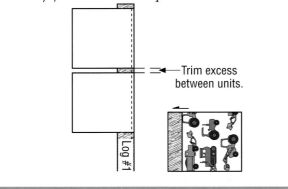

2. With Log #1 closest to you, place the center units on top of the strip for Log #2, right sides together. Position the units next to each other without overlapping the edges. Stitch. Cut between the units, trimming any excess fabric.

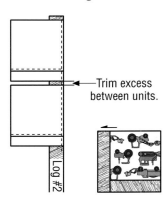

3. With Log #2 closest to you, place the center units on top of the strip for Log #3, right sides together. Position the units next to each other without overlapping the edges. Stitch. Cut between the units, trimming any excess fabric.

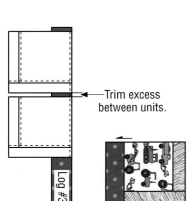

4. Continue adding logs in numerical order as shown to complete 6 Off-Center Log Cabin blocks.

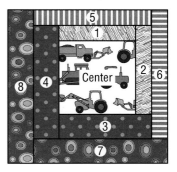

Make 6.

5. Arrange the blocks as shown.

6. Join the blocks in horizontal rows. Press the seams in opposite directions from row to row. Join the rows, making sure to match the seams between the blocks.

Quilt Finishing

Refer to "Finishing the Quilt" on pages 10–16.

1. Sew the inner border strips to the side edges of the quilt top first, then to the top and bottom.
2. Sew the outer border strips to the side edges first. Add a corner square to each end of the remaining outer border strips, then stitch them to the top and bottom edges.

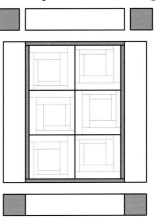

3. Layer the quilt top with batting and backing; baste. Quilt as desired.
4. Bind the edges. Label your quilt.

Dinosaurs Love Veggies

Color Photo: page 28
Quilt Size: 44" x 54"
Finished Block Size: 10" x 10"

Scotch Quilt Block
Make 12.

Materials		Cutting			
44"-wide fabric		**Cut all strips across the fabric width.**			
		First Cut		**Second Cut**	
Fabric	**Yardage**	**No. of Strips**	**Strip Size**	**No. of Pieces**	**Piece Size**
Theme print	½ yd.	2	6½" x 42"		
Fabric A	⅜ yd.	2	2½" x 42"		
		1	6½" x 42"		
Fabric B	⅛ yd.	1	2½" x 42"		
Fabric C	⅝ yd.	1	8½" x 42"		
		1	8½" x 42"	12	2½" x 8½"
Fabric D	⅛ yd.	1	2½" x 42"		
Inner border	¼ yd.				
(sides)		2	1½" x 40½"		
(top/bottom)		2	1½" x 32½"		
Outer border	1 yd.				
(sides)		2	6¼" x 42½"*		
(top/bottom)		2	6¼" x 32½"		
Corner squares	¼ yd.	1	6¼" x 42"	4	6¼" x 6¼"
Backing	2¾ yds. (pieced crosswise)				
Binding	⅜ yd.	5	2¼" x 42"		

*If your fabric is not 42½" wide, cut an extra strip and piece the side borders.

Quilt Top Assembly

1. Make 2 of Strip Set #1 as shown. Make 1 each of Strip Sets #2 and #3. From Strip Set #1, cut a total of 12 segments, each 6½" wide. From each of Strip Sets #2 and #3, cut 12 segments, each 2½" wide.

2. Make 12 Scotch Quilt blocks as shown. Press the last seam away from the center square in 6 blocks, and toward the center square in the remaining 6 blocks.

Cut 12.

6½"

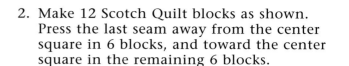

Theme print

Fabric A

Strip Set #1
Make 2.

2½"

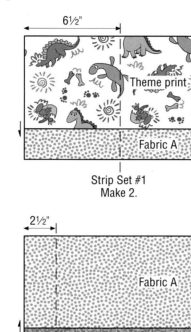

Fabric A

Fabric B

Cut 12.

Strip Set #2
Make 1.

2½"

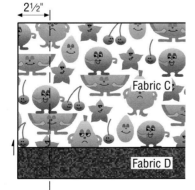

Fabric C

Fabric D

Cut 12.

Strip Set #3
Make 1.

Press this seam toward
the center square
on 6 blocks, and away
from the center square
on the remaining 6 blocks.

2½" x 8½"

Make 12.

3. Arrange the blocks as shown so the longest vertical seams are pressed in opposite directions when the rows are joined.

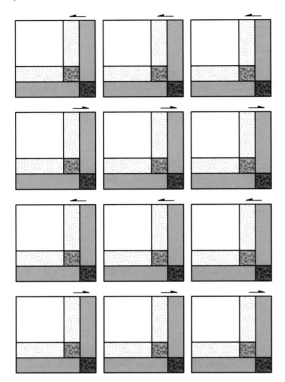

4. Join the blocks in horizontal rows. Press the seams in opposite directions from row to row. Join the rows, making sure to match the seams between the blocks.

Quilt Finishing

Refer to "Finishing the Quilt" on pages 10–16.
1. Sew the inner border strips to the side edges of the quilt top first, then to the top and bottom.
2. Sew the outer border strips to the side edges first. Add a corner square to each end of the remaining outer border strips, then stitch them to the top and bottom edges.

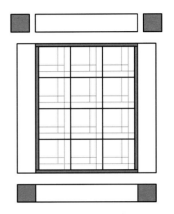

3. Layer the quilt top with batting and backing; baste. Quilt as desired.
4. Bind the edges. Label your quilt.

Lunchtime!

Color Photo: page 17
Quilt Size: 56½" x 72½"
Finished Block Size: 8" x 8"

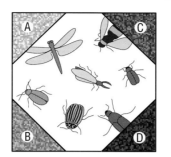

Snowball Block
Make 17.

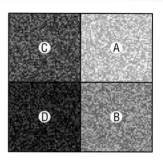

Four Patch Block
Make 22.

Materials
44"-wide fabric

Cutting
Cut all strips across the fabric width unless otherwise indicated.

Fabric	Yardage	First Cut		Second Cut	
		No. of Strips	Strip Size	No. of Pieces	Piece Size
Theme print	1⅜ yds.	5	8½" x 42"	17	8½" x 8½"
Fabric A	⅔ yd.	2	3½" x 42"	17	3½" x 3½"
		3	4½" x 42"		
Fabric B	⅔ yd.	2	3½" x 42"	17	3½" x 3½"
		3	4½" x 42"		
Fabric C	⅔ yd.	2	3½" x 42"	17	3½" x 3½"
		3	4½" x 42"		
Fabric D	⅔ yd.	2	3½" x 42"	17	3½" x 3½"
		3	4½" x 42"		
Inner border	⅜ yd.	5	1½" x 42"		
		2	2" x 42"	8	2" x 8½"
Outer border	1⅝ yds.*	2	7½" x 37½"		
		2	7½" x 53½"		
Backing	3½ yds. (pieced crosswise)				
Binding	½ yd.	7	2¼" x 42"		

*Cut strips from the lengthwise grain of fabric.

Quilt Top Assembly

1. Draw a diagonal line from corner to corner on the wrong side of each 3½" square.

2. Place a 3½" square on each corner of an 8½" theme print square, right sides together, as shown. Pay careful attention to the placement of the squares. Stitch on the drawn lines. Trim, leaving a ¼"-wide seam allowance. Press the triangles toward the corner.

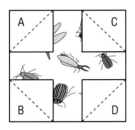 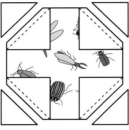

Stitch.   Trim.

Make 17.

3. Make 3 each of Strip Sets #1 and #2 as shown. Cut a total of 22 segments, each 4½" wide, from each of Strip Sets #1 and #2.

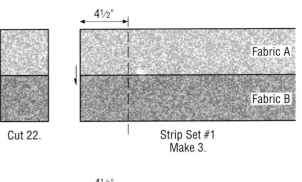

Cut 22.   Strip Set #1
Make 3.

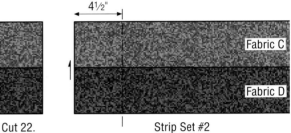

Cut 22.   Strip Set #2
Make 3.

4. Join 2 segments, 1 from each strip set, as shown to make a Four Patch block.

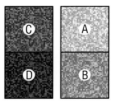 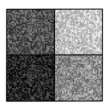

Make 22.

5. Arrange the blocks, alternating the Snowball and Four Patch blocks in each row, as shown. Be sure to match the fabrics in adjacent blocks. Reserve 4 Four Patch blocks for the corner squares.

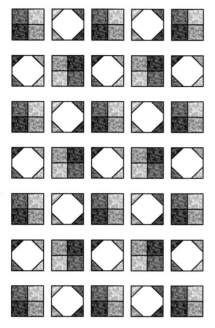

6. Join the blocks in horizontal rows. Press the seams toward the Four Patch blocks. Join the rows, matching the seams between the blocks.

Quilt Finishing

Refer to "Finishing the Quilt" on pages 10–16.

1. Join 3 inner border strips end to end to make one long continuous strip. From the long strip, cut 2 strips, each 53½" long, for the side borders. Trim each of the 2 remaining inner border strips to 37½" long for the top and bottom.

2. Join the inner and outer border strips as shown. Add a 2" x 8½" strip cut from the inner border fabric to each end of the border strips.

3. Sew the pieced border strips to the side edges of the quilt top first. Add a Four Patch block to each end of the remaining pieced border strips and sew them to the top and bottom edges.

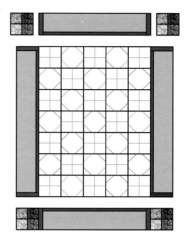

4. Layer the quilt top with batting and backing; baste. Quilt as desired.
5. Bind the edges. Label your quilt.

2 x 8½"   1½" wide   2 x 8½"

7½" wide

Make 2 for side borders.
Make 2 for top and bottom borders.

Junk Food Junkie

Color Photo: page 22
Quilt Size: 45½" x 56"
Finished Block Size: 10½" x 10½"

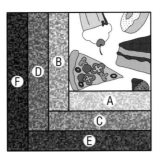

Chevron Log Cabin Block
Make 12.

Materials 44"-wide fabric		Cutting Cut all strips across the fabric width unless otherwise indicated.			
		First Cut		**Second Cut**	
Fabric	**Yardage**	**No. of Strips**	**Strip Size**	**No. of Pieces**	**Piece Size**
Theme print	½ yd.*	2	6½" x 42"		
Fabric A	¼ yd.	2	2" x 42"		
Fabric B	¼ yd.	3	2" x 42"		
Fabric C	¼ yd.	3	2" x 42"		
Fabric D	¼ yd.	3	2" x 42"		
Fabric E (top inner border)	⅓ yd.	3 1	2" x 42" 2" x 33½"		
Fabric F (right inner border)	⅜ yd.	4 1	2" x 42" 2" x 42½"		
Outer border (sides) (top/bottom)	1⅜ yds.**	 2 2	 6½" x 44" 6½" x 33½"		
Corner squares	¼ yd.	1	6½" x 42"	4	6½" x 6½"
Backing	2⅞ yds. (pieced crosswise)				
Binding	⅜ yd.	5	2¼" x 42"		

*You will need additional yardage if you want to center specific designs within each square.
**Cut strips from the lengthwise grain of the fabric.

Quilt Top Assembly

1. To quick-piece the center square and the first log, make 2 strip sets as shown. From the strip sets, cut a total of 12 segments, each 6½" wide.

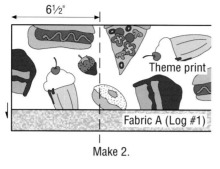

Cut 12.

Make 2.

> ### Note
>
> *If you cut the 6½" squares individually to center specific designs, you will not be able to do step 1. See note on page 67 for additional directions.*

2. With Log #1 closest to you, place the center units on top of the strip for Log #2, right sides together. Position the units next to each other without overlapping the edges. Stitch. Cut between the units, trimming any excess fabric between the units.

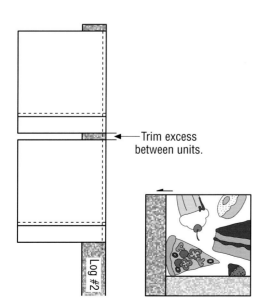

3. With Log #2 away from you, place the center units on top of the strip for Log #3, right sides together. Position the units next to each other without overlapping the edges. Stitch. Cut between the units, trimming any excess fabric between the units.

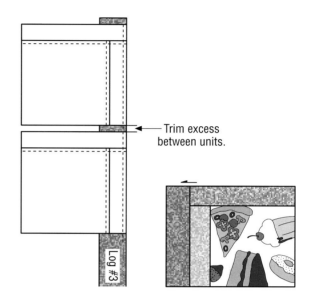

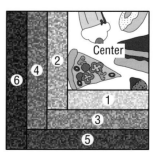

4. Continue adding logs in numerical order as described above to complete 12 Chevron Log Cabin blocks. When placing units on top of the long strips, position Logs #1, #3, and #5 closest to you, and Logs #2, #4, and #6 away from you.

Make 12.

5. Arrange the blocks as shown.

6. Join the blocks in horizontal rows. Press the seams in opposite directions from row to row. Join the rows, making sure to match the seams between the blocks.

Quilt Finishing

Refer to "Finishing the Quilt" on pages 10–16.
1. Sew the Fabric F inner border strip to the right side of the quilt top first, then add the Fabric E inner border strip to the top edge. The other two edges do not have an inner border.

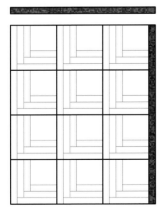

2. Sew the outer border strips to the side edges first. Add a corner square to each end of the remaining outer border strips, then stitch them to the top and bottom edges.

3. Layer the quilt top with batting and backing; baste. Quilt as desired.
4. Bind the edges. Label your quilt.

Laura's Quilt

Color Photo: page 21
Quilt Size: 50½" x 50¼"
Finished Block Size: 11" x 10¼"

The large animal print used in this quilt is the kind of fabric I love–it's bright, colorful, and covered with whimsical animal motifs. But it's not an easy fabric to use. Since the motifs are different sizes, they are difficult to combine in a setting.

First, I cut out each of the motifs I wanted to include in the quilt, adding a ¼"-wide seam allowance all around. I selected nine motifs and didn't worry that the lines around the motifs weren't straight. Second, I arranged the individual motifs on my design wall in three rows of three motifs each. The motifs varied greatly in size and needed some separation. To sew them together easily, it became clear I would have to make them all a uniform size. I decided to add strips of fabric around each motif, then trim

them all to the same size. Finally, I joined them with sashing strips, then added inner, middle, and outer borders.

Read through the following directions to see how I determined the uniform size of my blocks. Once you see how easy it is, you can apply this method to your own fabric. The yardage requirements and cutting directions provided are for the size quilt I made. Use them as rough guidelines only. Your requirements will vary, depending on the size of your motifs, the finished block size you want, and the number of blocks you intend to make. For example, I needed one yard of the large print to fussy-cut the nine motifs for my quilt. You may need more or less, depending on the size and number of motifs in your fabric.

Materials		Cutting	
44"-wide fabric		Cut all strips across the fabric width unless otherwise indicated.	
Fabric	**Yardage**	**No. of Strips**	**Strip Size**
Large print	1 yd.		
Background	¾ yd.	5	3½" x 42"
		3	2" x 42"
Sashing/Inner border	½ yd.	8	2" x 42"
Middle border	¼ yd.	4	1" x 42"
Outer border	1½ yds.*		
(sides)		2	6½" x 40"
(top/bottom)		2	7½" x 50½"
Backing	3⅛ yds.		
Binding	⅜ yd.	5	2¼" x 42"

*Cut strips from the lengthwise grain of fabric.

Quilt Top Assembly

1. Fussy-cut the motifs from the large print, adding ¼"-wide seam allowances all around. Arrange the motifs on your design wall.

2. Determine the length and width of your finished blocks. Start with the tallest and widest motifs and assume that you will have at least 1" of background on each side at the tallest and widest points. Anything less than 1" looks skimpy.

For example:
- Add 1" + 1" to the height of the tallest motif.
- Add 1" + 1" to the width of the widest motif.

   The size of my block needed to be at least 10¼" x 11" finished, or 10¾" x 11½" with seam allowances.

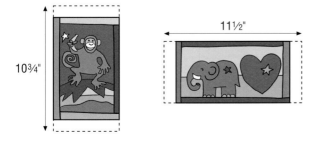

3. Use the smallest motif to determine the size of the widest strips needed to make the finished block size you determined in step 2. For example: my block will be 11½" x 10¾" including seam allowances.
- Subtract the height of the motif from 10¾" and divide by 2. This is the minimum width of the top and bottom strips.
- Subtract the width of the motif from 11½" and divide by 2. This is the minimum width of the side strips.

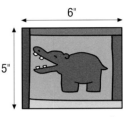

Width: 11½" – 6" = 5½"
5½" ÷ 2 = 2¾"

Height: 10¾" – 5" = 5¾"
5¾" ÷ 2 = 2⅞"

- After adding ½" to 1" for seam allowances and a fudge factor in case I changed my mind about the finished size of the blocks, I cut my wide strips 3½" wide.

4. To determine the width of the narrow strips needed to make the finished block size, use the tallest or widest motif. Perform the same calculations as in step 3.

Height: 10¾" – 8½" = 2¼"
2¼" ÷ 2 = 1⅛"

- Adding ½" to 1" for seam allowances and fudge factor, I cut the strips 2" wide.

Note

I did not perform these calculations for each motif. Since I determined the minimum widths for the largest and smallest blocks, the strips I cut worked for everything else in between. The excess was removed when I trimmed the blocks to size.

5. From background fabric, cut strips according to your calculations. You only need to cut strips in 2 different widths: 1 for the wider areas and 1 for the narrower areas. I cut 5 strips, each 3½" x 42", and 3 strips, each 2" x 42".

6. Sew the appropriate-size strips to opposite sides of the motif. Repeat with the remaining sides. Add strips to all your motifs. Double-check before adding strips to make sure you will achieve the desired size.

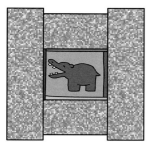
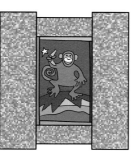

7. Trim the blocks to the required size plus ¼"-wide seam allowances all around. Use masking tape to mark the size of your block on a 12½" square ruler. (I placed tape at the 10¾" mark horizontally and at the 11½" mark vertically.) Place the ruler on top of a block, centering the

motif within the marked area. Trim the first 2 sides. Turn the block around and align the marks on the ruler with the newly cut edges of the block. Trim the remaining 2 sides.

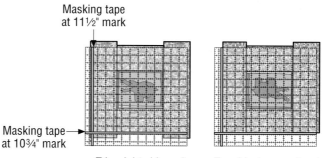

Masking tape at 11½" mark

Masking tape at 10¾" mark

Trim right side and top edge of block.

Turn block around and trim remaining sides.

8. Cut vertical sashing strips the same size as the length of your blocks. Remember to include seam allowances.

9. Arrange the blocks and sashing strips as shown.

10. Join the blocks and sashing strips in horizontal rows. Press the seams toward the sashing strips.

11. Measure the rows and cut 4 horizontal sashing strips to match.

12. Join the rows, adding a sashing strip between the rows.

Quilt Finishing

Refer to "Finishing the Quilt" on pages 10–16.

1. Sew the inner border strips to the side edges first, then to the top and bottom. Repeat with middle and outer borders.

2. Layer the quilt top with batting and backing; baste. Quilt as desired.
3. Bind the edges. Label your quilt.

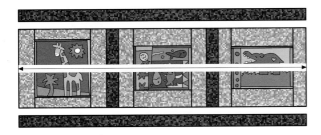

About the Author

There were no rotary cutters and very few quick-piecing methods when Ursula started quilting almost twenty years ago. Now she takes advantage of all the timesaving techniques she can to make quilts for friends. Like her first book, *Quilts for Baby: Easy as ABC*, this book was written for all quilters who enjoy making quilts but don't have much time to spend making them.

When Ursula isn't working as a technical editor for Martingale & Company, she's enjoying life with her husband, John, in the Red Rock canyons of southern Utah.